The Essential Toolbox for the First-time Leader

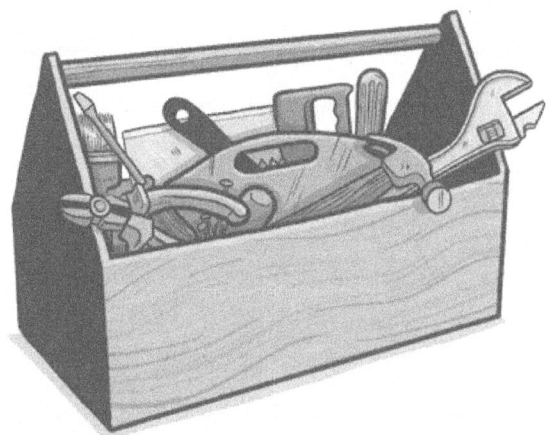

A set of practical, easy-to-use tips and hints for those of you
who are great at your job, but haven't led a team before.

FRODE SVENSEN
with Lori Shook

The Essential Toolbox for the First-time Leader

www.shooksvensen.com

frode@shooksvensen.com

+44 758 298 4479

Other books by Frode Svensen & Lori Shook:

TeamUp! Applying lessons from neuroscience to improve Collaboration, Innovation and Results

We wrote a book to show how you can base team development on neuroscience. We follow a fictitious – yet very real - management team as they learn and grow through a culture change programme.

To Lars, Eirik, Maren and Morten.
It's your turn now.

Table of Contents

About the author

I have been a leader most of my adult life. My first real leadership challenge was when I served in the Norwegian Navy. After my recruit school, I joined a five-month Quartermaster course and soon found myself in charge of a platoon of 48 guys of my own age.

It was my first attempt at being the boss, and somehow I handled it. The structure of the Navy helped, of course, as the formal hierarchy gave me some implicit power, but I also understood that I had to choose to be the leader. At the time, I decided to concentrate on one topic only: Make sure all 48 guys survive at the shooting range. No accidents. So I had a focus: Everything to do with weapons was priority number one, all else was secondary. We did not win any contests for the best-groomed platoon, (or any other contests), but we had no accidents and I was happy about that.

So I guess I learned Choose what you focus on.

A couple of years later I was a supervisor in Esso Norway, the oil company. I was in the IT user support department, and thinking back, this is where I made most of my mistakes as a leader. I was in charge of five or six people, all of them with more experience or better education than myself, and I had no further leadership training. Our group was swamped with requests from the IT users in the company, and I struggled.

I tried to choose what to focus on and found I couldn't decide. There were just too many requests and I spent too many hours delivering help instead of leading. I wish someone had helped me at the time to clarify my responsibilities, create effective processes, and take better care of my team members. Our group definitely delivered at our best when we spent time talking about what we all needed in order to become a better team.

It took me a couple of years and many mistakes to clarify my second rule *Let your team help you lead them.*

Fast forward some years and I was a leader in Capgemini, the IT and management consultant company. I was managing an office with about 60 consultants from all service lines: management consultants, IT consultants and outsourcing personnel.

As a leader in those five years I was able to choose my focus, and I decided that the most important job was to create what I called "accountable employees". I did not want millimetre justice, or too many rules; I wanted people to have generosity in their job and to support each other. By now, I was also quite good at getting help from my team in how they wanted to be led. A lot of the material for this book comes from my time there.

The next rule I learned was *Change takes time.*

Too often I believed that my splendid idea (which I had explained clearly at the monthly meeting) was going to be implemented immediately. That usually didn't happen. I now know that it takes time for people to make changes. If they buy in.

Will there be more rules that I develop? Most certainly. In my current work as a leadership trainer, executive coach and team coach, I get to work with a lot of leaders and I keep learning from them. I deeply appreciate the great conversations that I get to have with these dedicated professionals; their challenges and the solutions we find together continue to grow me. These conversations help me stay up to date with understanding current challenges that leaders face, which also supports me in training future leaders and, of course, it provides material for this book.

Introduction

I wish I'd had a book like this when I started as a leader. Either I didn't look hard enough or there really weren't any around. So I fumbled and stumbled and made it up as I went along. I made a lot of mistakes, as we all do, and recently I wondered: *Is it possible to collect some of my own experiences into a book that will be useful for a first time leader?*

I am passionate about creating more humanity in the workplace. So when I think of leadership, I think about the type of leader that creates connection to his/her people, where the leaders' behaviours create engagement and satisfaction in teams and throughout the organisation.

I hope you find something in here that will help you avoid some of the mistakes I made, and I hope these tips will help you to be more engaged and have your people be more engaged and happy at work.

I have written with several versions of you, the leader, in mind:

- You have not yet taken on your leader role, but your boss has asked you to take it and you're thinking: "Wow - how can I possibly survive as a leader?"
- You have just stepped into your first leadership role without much training or guidance and it is a pretty scary place to be.
- You have been doing OK for a while and you want more than to just get by, both for yourself and your team's sake. You want some tips and tricks that will make your days easier.

I have started with a section on **Knowing Yourself**, as I believe it is easier to do your job if you know who you are. It is also easier to understand others if you understand yourself first. In that part you will also find the theoretical stuff about how our brain works, how we are triggered by others, and how we can calm ourselves and others down.

I believe leadership is about relationships, so the section on **Great Conversations** is all about how to improve conversations with the people around you.

In section 3: **You as a leader,** you'll find tips on how to work with your team, and in section 4: **Making your day job easier**, I have collected my take on some of the "general knowledge" from leadership literature.

All the content of this book falls into one of these categories:

- **Personal experience:** I learned it, tried it out and found that it was helpful, or I learned from a mistake.
- **Through my clients:** During many conversations with coaching clients or course participants, I have learned through their challenges, and we found solutions that I present here.

I wish you all the best in your leadership journey and I would love to hear from you. Maybe there are topics you want more of (in the next edition), maybe you have a question or comment on some of the topics in this book, or maybe you just want to give me some feedback.

frode@shooksvensen.com

When you start

One day your boss asks you to take your very first leader position.

You might be "coming from the group", that is, asked to lead the group you are a member of, or you may be promoted into taking a leader position in another group.

In general, I have found that people want to help us, but it is so difficult for us to ask for help. My suggestion is to assume that the people around you want you to succeed, so ask them for assistance.

Make a plan for your transition. Make your plan fact-based and with SMART targets.

Firstly, it is a good idea to have some talks with your old boss and your new one, your peers and your direct reports.

From your old boss, you want to know things like:

- How can I use my previous knowledge in the new role?
- What should I look out for? What are the pitfalls for me?
- What do you think should be in my transition plan?
- How can you support me? Who else should I talk to?

With your new boss, you want to know:

- What do you expect from me? What are my day-to-day responsibilities?
- What should I do first? What is the biggest challenge?
- What are three things I could do to help you?

Talk with your peers:

- What are your expectations, advice or guidance?
- What are our responsibilities?

Talk with your direct reports:

- What is your job? What do you need in order to do it well?
- What are your strengths? And weaknesses? How can I help?
- What is a good leader for you? What else do you need from your leader?

Continue to create healthy relationships with your manager, peers and direct reports. Be professional in your stakeholder management. Document the conversations you have. Keep a list such as:

- Who I talked to
- What I learned
- How I will use this.

In order to be more easily accepted by the team, look for ways of creating some quick wins. Make sure that they are team wins, not individual wins. Publish these wins (as appropriate in your organization).

The Rules for being Human

When I first read the following, my reaction was that it was "just a poem". I typically don't read much poetry, and certainly didn't think I could learn from it. I was wrong. I like the sayings here, and it reminds me that I can learn and improve, and I don't have to be afraid of mistakes.

It also reminds me that I'm good enough, I can get better, and I have what it takes to be a good leader.

I invite you to read this through, more than once, and see if you can glean a few bits of wisdom for your own life and work.

Seneca Wolf Clan Teaching Lodge

You will receive a body. You may like or hate it, but it will be yours for the entire period, this time around.

You will learn lessons. You are enrolled in a full-time, informal school called LIFE. Each day in this school, you will have the opportunity to learn lessons. You may like the lessons, or think them irrelevant and stupid.

There are no mistakes, only lessons. Growth is a process of trial and error experimentation. The "failed" experiments are as much a part of the process as the experiment that ultimately "works".

A lesson is repeated until learned. A lesson will be presented to you in various forms until you have learned it. When you have learned it, you can go to the next lesson.

Learning lessons does not end. There is no part of life that does not contain lessons. If you are alive, there are lessons to be learned.

"There" is no better than "Here." When your "there" has become "here," you will simply obtain another "there" that will again look better than "here".

Others are merely mirrors of you. You cannot love or hate something about another person unless they reflect something you love or hate about yourself.

What you make of your life is up to you. You have all the tools and resources you need. What you do with them is up to you. The choice is up to you.

Your answers lie inside you. The answers to life's questions lie inside of you. All you need to do is look, listen and trust.

You will forget all of this

or

You can remember it whenever you want.

Section 1
Knowing Yourself and Your Brain

Understanding ourselves, how we function and why we react the way we do, is invaluable. When you learn something about your own leadership, you may find out that you want to change some of your behaviours. Change can be fun, easy and motivating - and it can also be challenging and hard.

Personally, I have always enjoyed doing self-assessment and personality tests. There are myriad tests available online. Some of them are just plain fun, some are more science-based and usually you can learn something about yourself. I suggest that you try one or more of them. You might discover something revolutionary that will rock your world, or you might just find a few useful insights.

My main message here is that in order to engage with other people, to understand them and to relate to them, it is very useful to know about yourself first and then look at the impact you have on others.

The first step is to notice: What am I doing and how does that work for me and for them? What is the outcome of those interactions? Do I create connection or distance? Do I inspire, or create fear?

The second step is to make some conscious choices about which behaviours we want to keep, and which we want to change or avoid.

Without that reflection, we blindly walk through life and let our habits and our unconsciously-generated emotions dictate what we do.

So let's dig in. Below, I offer a number of ways to get to know yourself – and some insights as to how your brain influences your behaviour.

Know yourself better with JOHARI

Here's a framework about understanding yourself - especially in relationship to others. This model, the JOHARI Window – and a tool by the same name - was created by Joseph Luft and Harry Ingham. JOHARI is a combination of their forenames. It also turns out that Johari is a Swahili word for jewel, and that's a happy coincidence as this model might be interpreted as a jewel discovery tool.

The model is about facts, qualities and behaviours that are known or unknown to you and others. It serves as a guide to help us consider how open, accessible and trustworthy we are in relationship to those around us. Joseph and Harry created a simple quadrant that looks like this:

JOHARI WINDOW

	KNOWN TO SELF	UNKNOWN TO SELF
KNOWN TO OTHERS	ARENA OR OPEN AREA	BLIND SPOT
UNKNOWN TO OTHERS	HIDDEN AREA	UNKNOWN AREA

The Arena or Open area:
This is what is known to you and known to others. You know that you have a particular expertise and others know this as well. You're not trying to hide anything and you are conscious and aware of the qualities or behaviours that you portray. We generally think this is a good thing – unless you're oversharing things that are not relevant.

The Hidden area:
There are things we know about ourselves that we are not willing or able to share (or haven't shared yet) with others. It's natural to withhold some facts, thoughts and fears about ourselves. We know it – they don't.

Here are a few examples of things that might be in the hidden square:

"I am uncertain about this proposal and I don't know how to handle it."

"I am definitely not an early riser, so I need some time alone in the morning before I engage."

"I want the boss's job."

The Blind spot:
There are things that others know about us but that we don't (yet) know. This is the "Bad Breath zone".

Examples:

"He often finishes my sentences. It's annoying but I don't think he realizes that."

"She really looks angry when she concentrates. It upsets people and she has no clue."

Unknown area:
There are things about us that nobody knows. We might endeavour to expand this area, but it might not be the first place we put our attention. Perhaps some great conversations could uncover some important jewels here.

Well, that's all well and good, but how do we use this model?

Generally, when working with this tool, the intention is to expand the Arena or Open area – especially around relevant qualities, characteristics and competencies. We can see that reducing the Hidden area or the Blind spot increases the Arena. This means that being more open (moving from Hidden to Open) or asking for feedback (moving from Blind spot to Open) is what we want.

Moving from Hidden to Open

It might be appropriate to hide some parts of your personal life in this area - I'm not suggesting that you start talking about your kids, cats or what you did on Saturday night after you left the pub. But what is it you know about yourself that would be helpful for others to know?

Maybe that you aren't a morning person and you just need that first cup of coffee before interacting with others. Or maybe that you are a little under-confident and you could do with a bit of help on something.

So, step one to expanding the known in a relevant and useful way is to reduce the Hidden area: Be open and transparent. Push yourself to be more open and sharing. Let people know more about you, your thoughts and your talents.

When working with me it is useful to know…

Here is another simple, easy and useful method that doesn't take much to implement. When people start working together, have them sit around the table and finish the sentence:

"When working with me, it's useful for you to know…"

My recommendation is that you do it often. At the start of a project is obvious, but how about at the start of a meeting? There might be something that is important for them to share today. How about as part of the Monday morning session?

Here are some examples I have heard:

When working with me, it's useful for you to know…

… that I need lots of detail in order to understand things, so I may ask a lot of questions.

… that I am NOT a morning person. I like to have a slow start and then catch up during the day.

… that I like to know WHY we do things – it is important for me to know the purpose if you want to engage me in your project.

… that I look angry when I concentrate to understand what you are saying. When I am angry, I will tell you.

… that I like to spend some time alone in my office after a meeting to recharge and to digest what I just learned.

… that I like the big, overall picture and I easily get lost in details.

We are all different. Telling each other about our differences can only help.

Moving from Blind spot to Open

Secondly, you can expand your Open area by finding out what others know about you that you don't. It is important that leaders demand feedback. Be curious, listen to what others have to say. You might be surprised to find you have some behaviours you weren't aware of that people either like or dislike. It will be helpful for you to know about these. If you want to create a learning culture or a feedback culture, you will need to go first.

Why is it important that you, as leader, go first?

You need to hear from your people what their anxieties are, what their concerns are, how they prefer to work, how they want to interact etc. Why should they be willing to share this with you if you don't share anything about yourself?

You must be able to give your people feedback to grow them. Why should they be willing to receive feedback if you are not?

This takes courage and it's worth it. Again and again, I've seen that a more trusting, transparent environment creates more positivity, engagement and ultimately better results in the team.

Copycats

More on moving from Blind spot to Open.

There is a video of my dad, me and my (then) six-year-old son walking away from the camera - side by side - down the street. It surprised me to see how I had copied my father's slight limp (from an old injury) and the way he held his arms behind his back. What was even more surprising was that my son had also copied this limp!

I guess I copied my father because I thought this was the way a grown man was supposed to walk – and that stuck. My son was just repeating the process. Copying is the most natural way to learn; it's human nature and it's often unconscious. I didn't decide consciously to walk the way my father did, but nevertheless, I saw it for myself – I was really walking with a slight limp!

When I became aware of that copycat walk, I could then make some other choices. Now I know that there are many different ways to walk and use my arms when walking. I can vary my posture and my stride when I want to – when I am conscious.

Watching the video helped me get feedback, so the way I walked was no longer a blind spot. If I hadn't seen this video, I would have continued to walk this way without knowing it.

Now I want you to view this copycat concept in two ways:

1. Who are you copying – consciously or unconsciously?
2. What do you want others to copy from you?

Who are you copying in your leadership role? How conscious are you about this process? Are you adding the little limps and anomalies that you saw in your first boss? Even the ones that don't make sense in your current circumstances?

The bosses you copy – were they the supportive, positive ones? Or the critical ones? What are some great qualities in leaders, teachers, or trainers that you've witnessed in your life and how could you copy them more consciously?

Thinking back to the Blind spot quadrant: How do you behave around others? How do you empower or develop them? When you're busy and focused on other things – when it's hard to pay close attention to your own behaviours – how do you behave?

The second question is possibly even scarier:

So, what are the ways that your people will copy from you and bring into their own leadership style?

I know they will copy you. You can choose to get more conscious about what you want them to copy.

If you haven't spent time thinking about this, it is a good idea to start spending some time reflecting (and getting feedback). Many of us are really good at capturing what we DID today and planning what we'll DO tomorrow. That is great, but here I am talking about what and who you ARE. It's a different focus.

What do you want to be remembered for?

I often ask my clients that question. It's a great exercise to get us to look at what is really important to us, and what we want to do with our lives. I strongly recommend you do it if you haven't already. Try to imagine what you want us to say about you when you are no longer here. It will probably get you in touch with your values.

Once in a while I meet clients who interpret the question a little differently and answer: "I don't want to be remembered".

This usually means that they – in humbleness and modesty – don't want us to put up a statue or plaque or memorial after them – they just want to be good people in this life. Something like that.

Sorry – but that is a choice you don't have. You will be remembered. The choice you do have is HOW. And it is by the actions of today that you can influence HOW we will remember you.

So the question is simple: Are your actions of today ensuring that people will remember you the way you really want them to remember you?

If not – what needs to change?

Trust and openness – a summary

In the previous chapters, I have deliberately *not* gone into a great debate of what it means to trust someone. Does trusting someone mean trusting them with your life? Your wallet? Your project?

I just used the definition from the Merriam-Webster dictionary: "Belief that someone or something is reliable, good, honest, effective, etc."

I consider myself a trusting person. For me, this means that I initially trust people, and they have to break the trust for me to mistrust them. Others hold trust differently. You may be suspicious of people until they have earned your trust. Both ways (or a combination of them) can work for us.

Either way, as a leader, you have to know that people follow you if they trust you and they trust you if they know you.

What we're really talking about is your trustworthiness – or how much others can trust you.

So this is my use of the JOHARI window: I want to stay conscious of how I increase the Open area by asking for feedback and by being appropriately transparent. This will make it easier for people around me to see the real me, and for me to see my blind spots, and more importantly – it will increase my trustworthiness.

I cannot control whether people choose to trust me or not; I can only control who I am as a person.

What is in your backpack?
- about reflection time

A lot of Leadership literature talks about the benefit of reflection time. Here's my talk:

You walk through life carrying two things: A briefcase and a backpack.

Your briefcase contains all that makes you a competent manager. The presentations, the spreadsheets, the calendar, the business knowledge, the budgets and the accounting, the white papers and the stakeholder analysis. And more. Everything is well organized, accessible and in file folders, so that you can easily have a look when you are on the move. Right now, the briefcase has the logo of your company on it.

Your backpack contains all that makes you a good leader. Your relationships, your experiences, your listening skills, your passion, your care, your delegation skills – all that makes you a decent human being. Everything in the backpack is a bit chaotic: it is not well organized and it's hard to find things when you need them in a hurry. You know that if you want to access what is in your backpack, you have to stop, sit down, take the backpack off, put it in front you and dig a little.

If you don't take time to reflect, you miss a lot of what you already have. When you go on leadership courses or read leadership literature, you're essentially filling up your backpack, but if you don't take time to use the knowledge, why bother? You are just carrying dead weight.

It is all there – you just have to search for it in your backpack.

Here is my challenge to you:

For the next three weeks, take 15 minutes every day to reflect? NOT while you're driving or cycling or doing anything else. Just while you're quietly sitting or walking on your own. Have a conversation with yourself about yourself. Ask questions like: "What have I learned so far in life about leadership? What is in MY backpack? How do I develop myself and my team?"

Some science about this:

To be able to learn, we have to be conscious about our learning.

When you've had a positive experience, one that you want to repeat, it helps to think about it. It helps to plan how to repeat it and be conscious about how to use the learning. If you've had a negative experience, it helps to think through how to avoid it or how to deal with the situation in a different way.

All this needs focus. You cannot think about everything else and focus on your learning at the same time.

So: Reflection time helps us learn.

Power is good
– balance is better

Many of you, as new leaders / supervisors / managers, face the same challenge: You are promoted to lead a team you have been a part of for some time, or you are promoted into a group of people who used to be colleagues in another team. Then you have to grapple with your new role as the leader of people you used to consider your peers.

So what do you do?

When I started out as a new leader, I went to both extremes: being "too tough" and being "too soft" at different times. It wasn't done consciously, and luckily I got some feedback from friendly people and took some time to reflect on my new role.

Now, as a trainer and coach I can see this happening again and again.

Some new leaders become too tough. They start acting with power and make VERY sure that no one is going to criticize them for being too soft and too friendly and too much "one of the guys". They stop going out with the friends they used to have in the team. They know that one day they may have to deliver a tough message, so they protect themselves by creating distance. They order, they control and they assess.

It's as if they are trying to be someone else, trying their best to play "the boss".

Does this sound familiar? Some version of this was me, when I started out as a supervisor.

It doesn't work. It's not authentic leadership.

Some new leaders become "too soft". They are so concerned about being seen as "the boss" that they overcompensate. They avoid conflict, they accept mediocre results and they even ignore flippant comments that undermine their authority. They don't dare assess people and they avoid giving them much-needed feedback. They hang out with the team after hours more than before, they Facebook-friend them and they neither lead nor manage their team. Whatever authority they had that made someone promote them is rapidly disappearing.

26

They are afraid of becoming unpopular. Their team gets away with disrespect.

It's as though they are trying to be who they were before the promotion and to play an impossible role: *"The circumstances and roles may have changed, but damned if I'm going to change my behaviour"*.

Does this sound familiar? Is this a version of you? Some version of this was also me, when I started as a supervisor.

It doesn't work. It isn't authentic leadership.

You took on the leader role for a reason. You actually do have a role to play in the team that is different from the other roles. A role of guidance, mentoring, coaching, managing, mediation etc. – all the things that great leaders do. And it includes giving straight feedback and sometimes assessing the performance of team members. It may also involve becoming unpopular at times.

So, welcome to leadership! It is POSSIBLE for you to be a leader. And it will work - if you lead. If you listen to your values and if you reflect. It helps to read and talk to your team about the new role, and to get mentoring, training, and coaching.

Whether you are a first-time leader or an experienced one, I guess you often have the challenge of balancing being "the buddy" and "the boss".

How do we get the balance right?

As the saying goes, "Be yourself – everybody else is taken".

Yeah, right, Frode. That is SO not helpful. When someone tells me to be myself, I go: "What???" Who knows who I am.

What I find helpful is taking time to reflect and to figure out what I want to do, what actions I want to take, so that I get to know myself better. It is great to have role models, but I cannot BE them. I have to do this my way. And I will make mistakes that I can learn from, if I let myself reflect.

This is why I strongly urge you to have reflection time. Yes, you do have the time, you just have to take it. 15-20 minutes each day without phones or any other disturbances.

Some of my clients ask me: "What am I supposed to do when I reflect? Don't I do enough planning and reviewing already?" I suggest they look in their backpack. And train themselves to find interesting questions to ask themselves about what kind of leader they want to be.

Two Beasts - which do you feed?

Let's dip into another aspect of the Hidden quadrant of the JOHARI model – or perhaps we'll venture into your Unknown quadrant.

There are a lot of internal conversations going on that you can become even more aware of. You might still choose not to share them – that's fine. But if you become more aware of your internal conversations, you can be more aware of your external behaviours and the level of stress you create for yourself.

This chapter is basically about self-esteem. My own self-esteem isn't always tip top. Sometimes I let myself listen to the inner critic or the negative chatter that tells me I'm not good enough. Other times I feel like a winner – I feel good about myself. The funny thing is, we can actually help ourselves to feel better about ourselves and develop self-esteem, by making one simple choice.

You may have read or heard this story in various versions. This is my coaching version.

There is one thing I know about you (and about me and everybody else):

You have two beasts living inside you.

Every time you think about yourself or talk about yourself, one of these beasts is fed. Every belief you have about yourself will feed one of these beasts.

One of the beasts is fed by thoughts like: I can't do that; I must do this; What will the neighbours say?; Who do I think I am?; I am weak or afraid or small; I have to do as I am told; I don't dare.

Find that beast inside you. What does it feel like? Look like? Sound like? What is its name?

The other beast is fed by thoughts like: I want to; I am good enough; I am strong; I am good at …; I CAN.

Find this beast inside you. What does it feel like? Look like? Sound like? What is its name?

Every time you have a thought about yourself, one of the beasts is fed, and every time it is fed, it grows stronger. And the stronger it becomes, the hungrier it gets.

Just try this:

Say out loud ONE thing that you know is true about yourself.

Did you notice which beast was fed? Did you hesitate about saying something out loud? Which beast was fed by the hesitation? Keep talking. Really, keep talking about yourself. Say something else that you know is true about yourself. And keep noticing which beast gets fed.

Maybe you have fed the beast that keeps you down a lot lately and it is strong and powerful and wants to be fed all the time. Start feeding the uplifting beast instead. In the beginning, you will notice that the negative beast raises its head and WANTS to get fed. It is POSSIBLE to practise talking to the positive one instead.

Maybe you have fed the positive one a lot lately and it is strong and powerful. Keep going. Notice when the other one wants to get fed

Become aware of which beast you're feeding and which beast is demanding to be fed in different circumstances. Remember – you get to choose!

Something you can do to increase your self-esteem

Research has shown that if you strike a "powerful pose", you actually change the chemicals in your body. So when you lift your arms above your head like a winner, or stand like Wonder Woman with your hands on your hips for just two minutes, the amount of testosterone in your system increases, which is good for self esteem and being assertive. The level of cortisol decreases, which lowers your stress level. So it is actually true that if you look like a winner, you feel like a winner!

False Positives and False Negatives

If we know how our brain works, it is easier to understand our own reactions. By understanding the following about how our brain scans the environment, constantly looking for threats and making sure that we are always ready in fight, flight or freeze mode, it becomes easier for us to understand what goes on in our relationships with other people.

We evolved as a species, Homo sapiens, on the savannahs in Africa. Those that survived, and therefore reproduced (and had their genes survive to end up in us), needed to be good at a few things:

- Finding food and avoiding poisonous stuff
- Avoiding being killed by predators
- Being social – so that their tribe mates liked them and helped them when they needed it.

Let us look at one of these features in detail: Early man needed to be good at differentiating between "friend" and "foe", at quickly identifying if something was a danger or not.

So imagine ... Early man is out there on the savannah. He sees something rustling in the grass and his brain, goes "Oh-oh, is this a danger?"

Supposing his brain very quickly decides that it is dangerous, gets into fight or flight mode (fills up with adrenalin etc.) and he does whatever is necessary to survive (climb a tree).

Now, if it really was a danger, he had a True Positive (meaning he was correct in assuming it was a predator) and he probably survived because he was able to run from the threat. If it turned out that it was just the grass rustling in the wind, he had a False Positive (meaning he was wrong in assuming it was a predator) and he survived - even if he might have been a little embarrassed about his overreaction.

On the other hand, if his brain quickly decided that it was not a predator – after all, he'd seen the grass move like this many times before - he probably told himself it was just the wind and continued his walk.

Now, if it really was a predator, his assumption of "no predator" was a False Negative and he probably died. If it was not a danger, he had a True Negative (he correctly assumed it was "no predator") and survived.

This tells us that it actually makes a lot of sense to have False Negatives about dangers: it is better to falsely assume that something out of the ordinary will hurt you, than to falsely assume that everything is fine. Early men that reacted quickly to a potential danger were better at surviving. And it didn't hurt too much to be wrong about that. But being wrong about the "it's safe" assumption could be deadly. Give this effect a few thousand generations to establish itself and voilà, here we are, very good at assuming that a stimulus might be a threat.

Why is this important? Because any time we are presented with a stimulus – a situation of any sort - our brain will very quickly try to figure out if it is a threat or not. The brain will actually assess it as a threat in five out of six cases: we are now wired to mostly perceive a stimulus as a threat, because millennia ago, it helped our ancestors to survive. We continue to do this regularly, but in our modern world it isn't as useful, as we will see.

Let us look at a classic example: You are giving a presentation and your boss is at the back of the room. Suddenly you notice that your boss is rolling her eyes. What happens with you? Your brain doesn't really know the difference between a physical threat and a social threat, so it immediately has a threat reaction: Your heart beats faster, your palms start sweating and your body is ready to fight or flee or even freeze. Your system is flooded with adrenalin and your mouth gets dry and... (you know the feeling). And all because your boss was following the flight of a fly in the room! You just had a False Negative as you wrongly assumed the worst:

Boss rolling eyes (rustle in the grass) = I am in trouble.

This gets compounded by the fact that the brain is always trying to justify our assumptions. We make assumptions all the time - it's a necessary part of daily functioning. And then we try to justify those assumptions.

Can you remember a time when you were certain, absolutely certain, that something was not going to go well? And then you found one little indication that it wouldn't go well? So you started to doubt the whole project? Maybe you were wrong. Maybe it was just a False Positive – remember, it's built in and it's less dangerous than assuming something will go right and it doesn't. The problem is that we can convince ourselves that something won't go well and actually tip it in that direction, or perhaps give up on an idea that contains some risk even if it's brilliant.

So, my advice is to think about your thoughts. Use reflection time, time-outs or whatever you call it to examine them: Is this really as bad as it seems? Am I just catastrophizing here? Is it just my limbic system giving me a False Positive?

Your brain has different parts

The following is a simplified explanation of the way the brain works, with just enough theory for our purpose: to understand how we can interact better.

While different authors and researchers have different models for the brain, it seems many of them classify our brain functions into two categories. For example:

- Neuroscientists talk about the *prefrontal cortex* controlling logic and conscious thought, and the *limbic system* as the centre of emotions.
- In his book "Thinking, Fast and Slow", Daniel Kahneman describes *System 1* and *System 2* and how they help us (or not!) to make better decisions.
- In "The Inner Game" books, Tim Gallwey talks about *Self 1* and *Self 2* and how they compete when we want to learn new skills.

The point - in all of the research – is that there are parts of the brain involved in conscious thinking, problem solving and logic, and other parts that deal with emotions, memory, and instincts.

My own way of describing this is: "My brain has many parts". Whenever I get an urge to act or react quickly, I know I need to stop and reconsider: there might just be an automatic reaction in one part of my brain that needs to be re-evaluated by another part.

First, let's look at the two regions that create the thinking fast vs thinking slow that Kahneman described.

The Limbic system:

The human limbic system evolved over millennia and is quite effective in its primary job of ensuring survival – but it's much more complicated than "eat but don't be eaten". We are social creatures and our survival is very dependent on our interactions with other people. The limbic system is itself a well-crafted instrument that is highly attuned to what goes on around us. When the limbic system perceives that something is a threat to our survival, it issues a fear response, causing us to react accordingly. If it decides that something is good for survival, it encourages us to go for more of it. In this way, the limbic system unconsciously, but powerfully, influences our behaviour through our emotions.

The Pre-Frontal Cortex (PFC):

This is the most evolved and sophisticated part of the brain. It has many functions including pointing attention, setting goals, using logic, making decisions, solving problems, seeing others' perspectives, delaying gratification and emotional regulation.

Unfortunately, the PFC is much slower than the limbic system, it burns up much more energy and it tires quickly. It is easy for the PFC to become tired and allow the limbic system to take charge, which means we are then making decisions based on emotion alone.

It takes work and practice, but we can train ourselves to keep the PFC in charge more often. It can still include emotions created by the limbic system, but we don't have to be run by those emotions.

Why do you need to know this stuff?

1. Understanding these brain functions and supporting your PFC will help you stay cool under pressure and make better decisions.
2. Realising that others also have a limbic system and are probably run by it will help you guide and lead them. Imagine that you have a magic formula that will help people be more motivated, and that you can remove or prevent some frustrations, reactions, resistance and revenge. It's pretty simple in the end – we just don't want to get others' limbic systems all riled up. The section on Be SAFE & Certain will dive into this more fully.
3. If you help other people to understand these different parts of the brain, you could help them to access their PFC more. This can create more possibility for a collaborative team culture. Limbic reactions are a fine way to disrupt trust, openness and teamwork. Tapping into PFCs together can radically increase your ability to collaborate.

In the next chapters, we will talk about some other parts of the brain and why it's useful to know about them. For now, let us look at a couple more ways you can use the knowledge about the limbic system and the PFC.

As a leader, you will constantly see yourself and your people being triggered by others. Being triggered is my way of saying: you see/hear something, you don't like what you see/hear, so you let the world know how displeased you are. Letting the world know takes many forms, from arching an eyebrow, rolling your eyes, making a flippant comment, to yelling, banging the desk or other physical manifestations.

The question, of course, is: "Do these reactions improve the relationship with your people or the culture in your group?"

If you know that they actually have a negative impact, then you can choose to do something about them. They are limbic reactions. Your limbic system has seen something that is *perceived as a threat* and therefore your body has been flooded with adrenalin and cortisol and you are ready to fight.

Your PFC was unaware, tired or not paying attention, and has therefore not stepped in with a more reasonable reaction.

So you need to give the PFC a chance to regain control over you. In the chapter about the ABC of Mindfulness, we talk some more about this, but for now, follow my grandmother's advice: "Count to ten - and breathe".

Allow the PFC to look at the situation: Is it as bad as it seemed, or are there more sensible ways to deal with the situation?

Moments of mindfulness are helpful – just sitting in a stress-free way and breathing for a couple of minutes. This will help you let go of instinctive fear responses and give you more space to respond with reason. Let yourself "think slow" rather than taking the fast response.

Be SAFE & Certain

Like a high-quality instrument, a high-performing team also requires regular maintenance and tuning. Without conscious attention and adjustments, teams will default to behaviours that destroy performance, behaviours such as strife, conflict, competition, petty grievances, blame and revenge.

The brain automatically and unconsciously generates destructive behaviours as part of its quest for survival. When we understand this quest better, we can reduce those negative tendencies and then choose behaviours that lead to high performance.

Here, we present a model to describe how the limbic system influences individual and team behaviours – both productive and destructive ones. We then offer a simple way to shift from survival-based behaviours to more productive ways of being and working together.

We have looked at the *limbic system* and the *Prefrontal Cortex.* We saw that when the limbic system perceives that something is a threat to our survival, it issues a fear response, causing us to react. If it decides that something is good for survival, it encourages us to go for more of it. In this way, the limbic system unconsciously but powerfully influences our behaviour.

Neuroscience research shows us that the limbic system is primarily focused on social factors. We name six of these social factors in the *Be SAFE & Certain model*: Belonging, Status, Autonomy, Fairness, Expectations and Certainty.

Monitoring these factors ensured the survival of humans on the savannah.

The limbic system is still using those same factors, even though the modern day world is a completely different environment. This sometimes creates surprisingly strong reactions to other people or events, leading to a spiral of reactions and ultimately, trouble.

Belonging – a sense of safety with others - of friend rather than foe.

We needed to belong to a tribe to stay safe and be cared for.

A sense of belonging helps a team form and creates the foundation for collaboration.

This was important for the early man, when survival depended on other people. We developed dopamine and oxytocin receptors to help us develop relationships.

Today, in our business environment, it is still important; we strive to belong, to fit in, to be liked and we are afraid of being "cast away".

A fear of being kicked out of the tribe will keep people from voicing an unpopular opinion, offering an innovative – but controversial - idea or sharing key information, e.g., that a project is headed off track.

As a leader, you can create more belonging in your team. Make sure that a newly-formed team is given a chance to create ways of working together that don't leave someone on the outside. It also helps if you get to know the team members, because different people will have different needs: someone may require lots of reassurance of belonging, for others that is just not so important.

Status is about relative importance to others and our place in the group.

Knowing one's place in the tribe created stability and strengthened the tribe.

When people feel relevant, special and needed, they are more likely to be positive, to contribute and to recognise others' contributions.

It was important for the early man to be relevant in the tribe, to know his position, his role and his worth. Not everybody needed to (or could) be the alpha-male, but all needed to know their place.

When individuals have an unfilled need for status they may become self-focused, critical of others or "ego-driven."

Today, in our business environment, we all feel better when roles are established, when we know how the (formal and informal) structures work, who is the boss and what our relationship to her is.

As a leader, you can help the team by establishing roles and responsibilities, especially in a relatively new team. Again, different folks need different focus.

Autonomy provides a sense of control over events.

At times we needed to be able to find new ways of doing things.

Autonomy allows for independent thinking and sets the stage for new ideas and innovation.

Even for the early man, it was important to have some autonomy – it was important for the survival of the species that some of the members of the tribe experimented, did extra-ordinary things, tried out new food sources, or even left the tribe to walk to Asia.

Micro-management and too many rules or restrictions can create low morale and possibly revenge.

Today, we feel annoyed if we are micro-managed, if there is no freedom to choose in the workplace. We see it express itself in the personalization of cubicles and choice of tie.

As a leader, your job is often to set goals, distribute work, delegate and manage. Spend some reflection time looking at how much the different team members need autonomy and how much support they need.

I will share my own story: I was promoted into a leader job and my previous manager was a classic micro-manager. I had hated the way he always meddled and checked my progress and told me in detail how to do things that I knew perfectly well how to handle. So I made up my mind that I was NOT going to be like that. My role was to give people lots of freedom, lots of opportunities to experiment and fail and I was there to support them if they needed.

After six months, productivity was low, half the people were very happy and the other half was seriously frustrated. Why? The experienced people loved the freedom, the autonomy and the way they were able to create within the boundaries of their projects. The inexperienced were just frustrated that I didn't give them enough direction, support or training, nor the feeling of being part of the team. They were left to themselves to "figure it out". Their limbic system were screaming: "I don't belong, I don't know what to do, I don't know my role and that feels very threatening".

With the help of a clever mentor and my own reflection, I realized that I could get what I wanted: "accountable employees", but I needed to give people enough belonging, status, autonomy, fairness and certainty, and not abandon them in the process.

Fairness is a perception of fair exchanges between people.

With a fair environment, more people survived.

A sense of unfairness (to self or others) creates a deep-seated emotional reaction and revenge.

People appreciate being treated fairly and are more likely to be generous in their contributions when a culture is fair.

We can see this is just as important in today's workplaces as it was on the savannah. It doesn't even have to be you who is treated unfairly; just watching someone else being treated unfairly gives us a bad feeling.

Neuro-biologically, the reaction of unfairness is very closely related to disgust – the same emotion as when we encountered rotten meat. So it's a strong emotion, and we spend lots of PFC energy to overcome it if we encounter it.

As a leader, it is important to know your own relationship to fairness. Does it mean that you must treat everybody the same? That they should have the same bonus and salary or reserved parking space? Whatever systems exist in your business environment, you need to understand that unfairness within the team can create very powerful emotions, leading to revenge and other dysfunctional behaviours.

Expectations – we are sensitive to disappointments.

We needed to be able to anticipate what would happen.

Meeting expectations creates stability. Exceeding expectations creates a reward response.

When expectations are not met, people experience (sometimes very strong) disappointment and emotional pain. This often happens because people make assumptions when information is lacking.

Notice what happens if you really expected something to happen and it didn't. Notice the disappointment. Many of us are so afraid of disappointment that we don't even let ourselves have the expectation. What will a lack of expectation lead to in your team? What will it do to your team's ability to be creative and fearless?

Notice that you probably expected a sentence here starting with "As a leader…"

Certainty concerns being able to predict the future.

We needed to know how to find sustenance and where danger lurked.

A sense of certainty helps people relax and trust. If their basic needs are met, they can more easily focus on tasks.

A lack of direction, vision or planning creates instability, lack of trust and discomfort. It might lead to a need in some people to over-control events and other people.

Different people have different needs. This goes for all the Be SAFE & Certain elements, including certainty. Some of your team members will feel very uncomfortable with uncertainty and will do all they can to establish certainty or a feeling of certainty, even to the extent of making up "facts" to feel like they are in control. Rumours start when information is missing.

As a leader, your job is to create a sense of certainty. How you do that is, of course, dependent on your situation. Even in the middle of a change program, where there are lots of unknowns, there might be some information that can be shared. Often just telling people what is unknown, and why, can help.

Summary of The Be SAFE & Certain model:

We are drawn towards reward and we avoid threats. We want more of Belonging, Status, Autonomy, Fairness, Expectations that are met, and Certainty. So if we are rewarded with more of these, we are drawn towards the person or situation that rewarded us with them.

If we feel threatened in any of these areas, we avoid the person or situation that threatened us.

As leaders of teams, we can do a lot to make our people feel rewarded and we can avoid making our people feel threatened.

Think of ways to make your people feel they Belong to the team, to raise or clarify their Status, give them Autonomy (within your constraints), treat them Fairly, meet their Expectations and give them as much Certainty as you can.

Different people have different needs; knowing your team members will help you create an environment where they will have fewer threat reactions and can feel safe and certain.

Mirror Neurons

Back in the 1980s, a group of scientists at the University of Parma, Italy conducted a series of experiments. They put electrodes in the macaque monkey brain and discovered which neurons were active in controlling the movement of hand and mouth.

It was a simple set-up: the monkey had electrical cords coming out of the brain which were connected to a machine that went "bing!" when the monkey picked up a nut from the table.

Now, imagine the scientists' curiosity when this happened:

The monkey was having a break, still wired to the machine, and one of the lab assistants picked up the nut from the table. The machine went "bing!"

Lots of research later, the scientific community seems to agree that some of the neurons they recorded activity from were responding not only when the monkey picked up the food itself, but also when it saw someone else pick up a piece of food.

Much more research is needed - and is happening – and some of the research gives us mixed messages, but it seems that mirror neurons (and other systems in the brain) could explain why I can "feel what you feel". Interesting?

Try looking at children laughing. It is almost impossible not to start laughing with them. (Emotions are contagious.)

Look at the child reaching for the cookie jar. You know that she wants cookies, right? (We understand others' intention.)

If I walk barefoot past the coffee table and you see me accidentally kick the table leg, you can literally feel the pain of my dislocated toe. (We feel others' pain.)

These examples may be mirror neurons in action.

This has implications for how people interact. Mirror neurons may explain a lot about how we can understand intention in others, why we have empathy for others, how we learn languages and more.

For us as leaders, it is useful to know that people around us are affected by our emotions.

Showing emotions

Now that you understand about mirror neurons, you have a choice:

You can choose to try to hide your emotions as best you can because you know that the team members are affected by your emotions and you want them to be professional about their job.

OR

You can choose to have your healthy emotions and show them - let people see you as a whole human being.

I strongly recommend the latter.

- You are not good at hiding emotions – no one is. On the other hand, most human beings are very good at interpreting other people's moods. If you try to "fake it", people will know and it will make it difficult for them to trust you.
- You set an example. The workplace needs more emotion, more humanity, not less. We don't want our people to leave their humanity at home in the morning and behave like automatons at work. If you want to have a trust-based environment, you want people to be honest, including honest about their feelings.

ABC of Mindfulness

Imagine that you become triggered because your limbic system perceives a threat. Your adrenalin and cortisol are flowing, your heart rate quickens, your palms start sweating, you are ready to fight!

Awareness - become aware of your reactions, adrenaline and stress chemicals. Just by taking a moment or two to be aware of what is happening in your brain and body, you will begin to reduce the impact of the limbic system's reactions.

This is the beginning of a mindful state. A focus on breathing will also help to strengthen mindfulness.

BREATHE

Breathe – breathe and relax the body to flush out stress chemicals and return to a balanced, neutral state. Then you can more easily observe events from a non-judgemental and more objective perspective.

Mindfulness is being aware of one's own thoughts and stepping out of judgements of right/wrong and good/bad – at least for a moment.

CHOOSE

Choose – Once we know how to recover from reactions, we have a choice about how we respond to people or events:

We can respond EITHER from a limbic, reactive state OR from the PFC, which is better able to reason, to see the whole picture, to embrace paradox, to delay gratification and to have empathy for others.

We can also choose to practise mindfulness. The more we experience this state, the more we are able to access it in the moment.

How you can help your teams be their best

Given its strong social nature, our brain gives us a powerful innate ability to work and create together with others.

But, if the limbic system is in charge, our social interactions are likely to be negative and destructive.

We need, instead, to rely on the prefrontal cortex, the most evolved and sophisticated part of the brain. It has many functions including pointing attention, setting goals, using logic, making decisions, solving problems, seeing others' perspectives, delaying gratification and emotional regulation.

Unfortunately, the prefrontal cortex is much slower than the limbic system, it burns up much more energy and it tires quickly. It is easy for the PFC to become tired and allow the limbic system to take charge.

It takes work and practice, but we can train ourselves to keep the prefrontal cortex in charge more often. It can still include emotions created by the limbic system but we don't have to be run by those emotions.

Helping people to understand these different parts of the brain and training them to access their PFC sets the stage for a collaborative team culture.

Reduce limbic reactions by learning to Be SAFE & Certain as much as possible. Reduce potential threats to people's belonging, ensure their status is intact, allow some autonomy, be fair, communicate well so people set realistic expectations, and create as much certainty as possible.

Teach teams to tap into their prefrontal cortex and use mindfulness - see the ABC steps.

Once teams are adept at using their prefrontal cortex together, they will have more ability to work through conflict or disagreements. The creative process will no longer be stopped by fear of conflict or fear of judgement.

Invite diverse viewpoints and learn to create from differences rather than trying to find common ground. If people are able to stay in their PFC, they can more easily entertain paradoxes and consider new thinking that might lead to innovative solutions.

Positivity, appreciation and gratitude are also helpful in developing teams that can co-create well together. These can generate oxytocin and build strong bonds between team members, leading to more trust and openness.

Section 2
Great Conversations

What do we mean by Great Conversations? What IS a Great Conversation?

You know it when you are in one. You feel you're being listened to, that the thoughts you express are respected and appreciated and built on and that others are interested in what you are saying. The people in the conversation walk away with a feeling of having understood something better, learnt something new, shifted a perspective and being better connected. It is not about who talks the most or least, who "wins" the argument or who gets convinced about something. There are only winners.

It is NOT a debate or argument. It is not measured by how eloquently you present your ideas and win others over. It is a conversation where there is no criticism, where you don't feel the need to defend yourself. There is no stonewalling ("silent treatment") or contempt ("eye rolling").

Sadly, we don't have many Great Conversations. We are not trained and socialized to have them. We have been taught to win arguments and play the political game. We are so used to punches and jabs and sarcasm that we may not even consciously notice them any more. All we notice is disconnect and loss.

The result is catastrophic in the workplace. People stop speaking up, they withhold information and they lose the courage to be creative – to express great ideas. We suffer through boring meetings where a few individuals "win" and most of us lose. Relationships break down (or up) and we lose great people because they don't feel respected, listened to and appreciated.

It is possible to change this. There are Skills, Tools and Training available.

This is not instead of all the good work that consultants do on your Change Programmes, or instead of the training your people need in order to learn new processes or skills. We need to learn how to have

Great Conversations to make sure that change programs and training succeed.

Imagine a time when the tribe went out in the field during the day. The more experienced members showed the newbies how to hunt and gather and make tools and weapons and how to use them. They trained and practised and shared feedback. In the evening they sat down around the campfire and talked and coached and shared experiences – they reflected in order to create new ideas for how to make life better. They had Great Conversations.

Your tribe (or organization, or team) can learn how to have Great Conversations.

Frame of Reference
- we are all different

How many conversations have you had that deteriorated to (a version of):

"Yes, it is!"

"No, it isn't!" ...?

Even with people in our own team. But surely we all have the same goals and see the world in the same way? Not true.

Some want to reduce cost, others want to build more business. Some think a team-building weekend is a great idea, others think it's a waste of time. Some believe that the ball is red, others claim it is orange.

How is it that we look at exactly the same situation, and we see completely different realities?

We are all different. Reality is not what IT is, reality is what YOU are. It is subjective.

We all have a different frame of reference. All I know is that my frame of reference is different from yours. I have a different set of beliefs, values, needs, education, culture (family, company or national culture) than you have. I probably have a different personality, possibly have a different religion and definitely have different experiences.

Everything that fits in my frame of reference is good. It feels comfortable and I see the benefit and it feels right. Anything that's outside my frame of reference is not good. It's bad or boring, alien or scary or hard to understand, and it feels wrong. Or I don't even see it at all!

So how can we work together, collaborate and co-create, when my world is so different from yours?

We need to find overlaps in our frames of reference. In every conversation, I have an opportunity to understand what goes on in your frame of reference. Not to convince or win but to understand. I need to be interested before being interesting.

Unless I understand what goes on in your frame of reference and WHY you have the opinion that you have, it's going to be very hard to collaborate with you.

We need to listen to understand.

Where is your box?

Have you ever been in a conversation where you KNOW that the other person is NOT listening? She is just waiting for you to finish your sentence so that she can counter with her arguments. She's doing what we call "reloading the gun". And she started her next sentence with "Yes, but..."

Have you ever been in a conversation where YOU have not been listening? And started your next sentence with: "Yes, BUT..."?

Of course. We all have.

When you walk into a conversation, you are carrying a box in front of you. In this box is your frame of reference, your point of view and all the arguments you have planned. The other person is carrying her box. Both of these boxes bump into each other and they get in the way of the conversation. If you only want to explain what is in your box and the other person is doing the same, what happens? Nobody listens.

You can only change yourself. So don't even start to think "If only the other would listen better, this conversation would be more fruitful". Just don't.

Imagine a small table beside you. It has a pristine tablecloth draped over it, it is solid and it is a nice place for boxes to be placed FOR A WHILE. Put your box there for a while. It will not disappear. It will not lose power and it will not change (unless you choose it to).

Now you are ready to be interested in the other person and in whatever is in her box. Explore. Ask questions. You want to understand. Will your box try to jump back into the conversation? Of course it will, and you notice it when you catch yourself saying "Yes, but..." When this happens, put your box back on the table – turn your attention back to the other person and listen to what she is saying. Ask more questions.

I hear you ask: "So what happened to my arguments – I have a job to do. I need to influence this person. When is she going to listen to what's in MY box?" Simple.

When you are interested in what's in her box. When you show that you want to understand WHY she's having her opinion, then she will be more interested in listening to what's in your box. But only then.

Listen to understand – put your box aside.

Know-Do-Feel

Sometimes we need to have what we think of as "a difficult conversation". Either we agree with the other that it's going to be difficult (sorting out a mess) or we just have a feeling from the other person's body language or recent behaviour - this is going to be "one of those conversations"…

Here's something that might help, three questions that can shape what you want to say.

After the conversation, what do you want the other person to:

*   KNOW?
*   DO?
*   FEEL?

What do you want them to KNOW?

It sounds very simple, but sometimes it takes some preparation. It's not always facts - like what time the work day starts here. It could be what impact this person has on others.

If you don't know what your message is – there is a high probability that the other person won't get it.

What do you want them to DO?

What action do you want the person to take as a result of the conversation?

If possible, formulate the "do this" in an algorithm like "WHEN that is the situation, THEN do this."

"Our meetings start on time" may be important to know. But it doesn't necessarily lead to an on-time arrival. "When the Monday morning meeting starts at 09:00, then I want you to make sure you're in your seat, ready to attend, coffee cup filled and phone turned off."

Another example: "When John asks a question in our staff meeting, then count to three before saying anything. See if anyone else has an answer before you jump in."

How do you want them to FEEL?

This is often the hard one. The good news is, you often don't need to, or even want to, articulate a clear response to this question. But you do need to answer it for yourself.

How do you want the person to feel? Sorry? Inspired? Appreciative of the gravity of the situation?

The Be SAFE & Certain model can help you think through this. When you want to influence someone, it may help you formulate your message in a way that doesn't push her away from you.

Using the examples above, let's say you, the leader, want the person to feel

- On notice!! You are sick of this behaviour. If it doesn't stop – NOW – they're cooked.
- Inspired. You like this person, want to see them fix the problem and soar.

Draft sample sentences and read them out loud from each "feeling."

It is not so much WHAT you say or do, but HOW.

Do you want to inspire your people?

What is your cathedral?

I walked into a quarry one day to interview people about their jobs. Side by side, two middle-aged men were sitting on stools cutting stone.

I asked the first man "How's your job?"

He looked at me and said: "You know, I quite possibly have the most mind-bogglingly boring job in the world. I have been sitting on this stool for about 25 years cutting two-by-two-by-fours and the supervisor is so picky about my measurements that he checks every single stone. There are no other jobs in this village and I am bored out of my mind!"

"Hmm", I said.

I asked the other man "How's your job?"

He looked at me and said: "You know, I quite possibly have the most inspiring job in the world. I have been sitting here on this stool for almost 25 years cutting two-by-two-by-fours and I take such pride in making them accurate. Every Sunday afternoon for the last 25 years I have taken my son down to the village square and I can point to every single stone that I have cut that was used to build the cathedral. My son has been so inspired that he decided to become a carpenter so that he will be the one putting the roof on the tower of the cathedral."

"Hmm", I said.

What is your job?

Is it producing reports and filling in spreadsheets, writing emails, making presentations or following up on projects? Is it cutting stone?

OR is it being part of an organization that creates something to make lives easier for people, or to make the world a safer place? Are you working for an organization that makes a positive contribution to the world?

You choose. It doesn't matter what the company or organization you work for really DOES, as long as you know WHAT the contribution is. If you think your job is to cut stone, it's going to be really difficult to inspire your own people. If you know which part of the cathedral you are delivering, it's going to be a lot easier.

So what is it? What is the cathedral or part of the cathedral that your organization is building?

To be inspiring, you must first be inspired.

And here's another view on inspiration. We often think of it as someone "on stage" who has a message for everybody, the rah-rah of inspirational speakers. Well, since this book is about working as a leader for a group of people, I believe that if you want to inspire your people, you must know **what** inspires them and **how** they want to be inspired. This, of course, you can find out by having a Great Conversation with them.

So: know what inspires you, know what the purpose of your job is, and know your people.

What if?

Here's a little tip that will improve the quality of your conversations:

Use "What if..." instead of "Why didn't you..."

There are situations where you look at behaviour from a team member (someone has done something) and in your opinion they should have done something else.

You want to correct them (without making too big a deal of it).

So you ask them: "Why didn't you..." or "Why haven't you..."

I guess what we REALLY want is for the person to look at possibilities. Unfortunately, we usually don't get that result; what happens is that the person gets defensive. Their brain has interpreted your question as a threat. Their limbic system goes: *"Oh, I must have done something wrong, I will be punished, I need to fight back or run away. I have stopped listening now and I'm certainly not looking for creative (alternative) solutions."*

It might actually help if you use the words: ***"What if..."***

Example – notice how different these sound:

Why didn't you write a short management summary in your report?

OR

What if you wrote a short management summary in your report?

Apologize

Very often in my work life and private life I make mistakes. I mess up, I say something that wasn't too smart, I just don't get it right and people get hurt. And I'm not especially good at saying "I'm sorry".

Do you recognize yourself in this?

If so, we need to practise more. Some of us believe that if we apologize, we lose face or lose power or let the other person win in some way.

I don't think so.

Apologizing to the other person is giving us both a possibility to start again.

It's sometimes hard and it sometimes feels weird and it touches upon the "losing face" aspect, and yet it is so powerful.

AND: on the other side – when somebody apologizes to you, accept it.

What's really going on here?

Anna tells Bob "your presentation really sucked and it wasn't helping me in the sales meeting."

Let's look at it through the Be SAFE & Certain model:

Anna has threatened Bob's status, (he feels belittled by "really sucked"), he feels treated unfairly (he worked hard on this presentation and now she dismisses it) and he feels uncertain about what consequences this will have. His brain may have all kinds of other negative reactions too.

Bob's brain notices the social threat; this provokes the amygdala, so he gets a surge of adrenalin and wants to attack or run away.

Anything Anna says in the next few minutes is either not heard by Bob, or else it is interpreted in a negative way: he is triggered.

Before Anna can do anything meaningful with Bob – like helping him make a better presentation in the future – she must remove the threat and get him un-triggered.

66

An easy way to do this is to say "I apologize for using those words; they were too harsh and I shouldn't have used them. I'm sorry."

Here's the challenge, though. If Anna doesn't mean it, Bob will definitely feel that she is insincere and that's probably just going to make him more triggered.

So: get over yourself and your pride and whatever it is that stops you from apologizing. And then, and only then, apologize.

Assume good intent

I believe that ninety percent of all the problems in the world are caused by misunderstanding.

Here is an attitude that will help you: *Assume good intent.*

People don't want to be bad or wrong or out to get you. When someone butts up against you and you get triggered by what they say or do – ask yourself what's happening in you, and listen to them.

For example, there are a number of reasons why people behave in a way that triggers me and makes me impatient, angry, irritated etc including:

- They have a different frame of reference so they see the world (slightly or completely) differently than I do
- They think I'm not listening to them
- They have a different opinion on the subject we're discussing, and they don't have a way of presenting it that serves the group
- They are triggered themselves by something I have said
- They have a lot of passion for the subject but it comes out in a negative way.

So the leadership I can show is to listen to understand.

Why is this so difficult? I believe one of the reasons is the way our brain is put together.

We now know that our brain really wants us to see stimuli as threats. So when someone in your team says: "I don't think we should do what you just suggested", your brain will see it as a threat. It will want you to be defensive. It will want you to re-establish your status, get certainty etc. So you consciously have to decide to "assume good intent" and get curious about what is in the other person's frame of reference.

Interruptions

Imagine the following situation:

You are standing in the office, having a conversation with Jimmy. Anna walks up, she does not acknowledge Jimmy, she addresses you directly. You answer her and turn your back at Jimmy and continue to talk to Anna.

You would think that was pretty rude, right? And that it's probably a very rare situation?

Wrong. It happens all the time – with the use of technology: the mobile phone.

Why is it that we allow this to happen? You're having a conversation with Jimmy, your phone rings and you take the call, interrupt the conversation with Jimmy and leave him standing there.

Why is it that the person on the phone is more important than the person you are having a conversation with?

I think it is just as rude as if the interruption happened face to face.

We let technology excuse behaviours that we wouldn't allow in person.

Be conscious about how, when and whom you interrupt.

Appreciations

Before my wife and I go to sleep we make sure we share a couple of "I love you because…" It is a nice little tradition to show what we appreciate about each other and I certainly like to hear her tell me out loud that she appreciated <whatever it is she has noticed that day>.

How do we do this in the workplace, where statements starting with "I love you because…" would probably be reported to HR?

In numerous courses that I have led, I have found an opportunity to create a small (or large) circle, have each person look at someone across the circle and just say "What I appreciate about you, (name), is …". No feedback, no criticism, no explanations. Just appreciation. It creates a wonderful boost of positivity.

What if we did more of this? What if you started doing it every Friday afternoon in your team? What would you create? What do you have to lose?

Assumptions

Here is a way of looking at assumptions.

You have probably seen this before:

ASS U ME

That's how you spell assume, and it translates to: "If you assume, you make an ass of you and me". Haha.

The theory is that we should be careful when making assumptions. I agree. Assumptions usually come from a part of our brain that makes quick decisions based on limited information and they are definitely not always correct.

More importantly, when I make an assumption about you, it often says a lot more about who I am than it does about you.

We cannot stop making assumptions. Our brain will make assumptions all the time. The sensible way to deal with that is to be aware of the assumptions you have made and check them out.

Another interesting exercise is to play *The Assumption Game*. Do this with a person you trust:

Sit down with him or her and share the assumptions you have about each other. It can lead to a Great Conversation. You get to hear what your friend believes is true about you and you may want to correct it. Or you get to understand more about this other person and how and why they made this assumption. It can be a great, vulnerable place for both of you and it can lead to more trust between you.

"Mind the gap"

If you have ever travelled on the London Underground ("the Tube") you have heard this message.

Now, let us look at some other gaps. First, a couple of classic examples:

The conversation with the boss is not as meaningful as you would like it to be. The boss always talks about the tasks, the targets, the business, and you want to have a deeper relationship with the human being. You are prepared to talk about feelings and emotions. The boss is not.

We work with people from different cultures, and one of the frequently mentioned gaps is whether people will engage in "chit-chat" before getting down to business. Typically (and stereotypically!) the German walks into your office and starts talking about the task at hand, while the Middle Easterner wants to have more of a relationship first.

And how about:

"Women want to talk about the problem, men want to solve it."

This is not The Truth. The foregoing are examples of Gaps between different Frames of Reference. People are different, but we'd like everybody else to be like us, talk like us and talk about the stuff that we want to talk about. So we get frustrated, angry, less motivated to have a Great Conversation, and then we judge the other person as being wrong. It is not helpful.

What tends to happen when we get frustrated by the lack of (others') understanding, is that we start blaming or getting defensive, we stonewall or we show our contempt. (These are "The Four Horsemen of the Apocalypse" that John Gottman has written extensively about).

Why are there these gaps in our ability to show emotions, to have better relationships and to allow humanity into the workplace? Why is there such a vast difference in people's emotional intelligence? We can look for these reasons in a lot of different places:

Successive generations have had massively different experiences in their formative years: war/no war; struggles and famine or abundance and luxury; varying standards of living and access to material goods; differing influences by parenting literature – and many others.

There are differences in national cultures, educational influences and training environments, not to mention a growing appreciation of gender differences. Let's just agree that there are differences and lots of reasons for these differences.

Let us be gentle with each other. Let us be curious about each other. Let us listen to understand.

We are all different and have different frames of reference. What if we accept that others cannot talk the way we talk, avoid blaming them for being wrong, and learn to explain what we need and want from the relationship? And accept that we sometimes cannot get everything we want.

Maybe your boss wants to have a different kind of conversation, but all her training and upbringing has not prepared her for having it. So she needs to learn, without being made wrong for not being good at it from the start. You need the courage to start a Great Conversation.

Maybe the guy from the other culture (country / department / company) has been a star in that culture and everything he does worked great over there. So maybe he hasn't quite understood that we do things differently here in this new environment. Maybe you need the courage to have a Great Conversation with him where you don't make him wrong.

Section 3
You as a leader

Even if I know that I made many mistakes when I set out as a leader, I also know that I was quite lucky. I was surrounded by people I could learn from. I had some mentors in the early years that helped me think through what was useful behaviour and what wasn't.

I had a father I could talk with about leadership issues; sometimes we agreed and sometimes he had very different perspectives on a situation.

The following section is a collection of practical tools that I find useful as a leader. They all made sense to me and I just wish I had learned to use them earlier.

Treat them as they want to be treated

In my culture there is a saying:

"Treat everyone the way you want to be treated."

I think it is wrong.

I prefer to say: "Treat everyone the way THEY want to be treated."

If you show respect to other people, you don't assume they want to be treated the way you like to be treated. You are curious about their frame of reference and you try your best to treat them the way *they* want to be treated.

Be interested – not interesting

A lot of us try to impress others. I guess it is human nature. But it is not leadership.

I'm sure we have all met the person who only talks about himself. He tells you stories that may be interesting, but after a while you get the feeling that he is not at all interested in *your* stories or comments.

There is a particularly annoying version of this in the person who always has to be "one up" on you. You tell a story about when you almost caught a 7-kilo salmon last year, and he has to wade in with a story of how he actually caught and landed a 12-kilo salmon.

So here's your challenge: You may actually have a better story or a bigger event to share. Think – be conscious: do you really have to tell your story now? Be supportive and interested in the other person's story. Your turn will come another day.

There is nothing more interesting than a person who is genuinely interested in you. Decide that you will be interested in the people working for you – and they will find you interesting.

So, if you want to impress others, have the courage to let them impress you. That's impressive!

Treat everyone as equals

This title is really obsolete, right? We all treat everyone as equals – or at least with the respect they deserve…

This entry is about what my father called "the invisible people" in the workplace: The people answering the phone (are there any of those still around?), the janitors, the mailman, the cleaning lady, the guy changing water cooler tanks, the driver, etc.

I learned very early on in my working career that by treating everyone as equals, I felt better AND it made business sense.

I used to spend some extra seconds chatting with the receptionist at a customer's office (a huge place with hundreds of people walking through the gates every day). One day I really needed a favour on my way to this customer (I'd forgotten to take some print-outs with me). I was able to call him up and ask for his help as a personal favour. Way out of his job description. Saved my day.

Another time, I was working for a BIG company: The mail-truck was ABSOLUTELY NOT to be borrowed by employees after hours. And still, we all knew that once in a while, the truck wasn't in the car park overnight. So SOMEBODY could borrow it. And when I asked for a favour because I really needed to move some boxes over an evening, it was suddenly possible to borrow it. Why? I had spent enough time chatting with the mail guy to create a relationship with him.

Simple, banal examples of what happens when you treat everyone as equals.

"Treat the invisible people as human and you will become more visible."

"The Leadership Code"

During the winter, many Norwegians go up into the mountains for cross-country skiing. It is – in most cases – a great outdoors experience, but in some cases, there are accidents and even fatalities, mostly because people don't follow some simple rules of conduct in the mountains and because of the fast-changing weather conditions. So for many years, the Norwegian Trekking Association has published and promoted the Norwegian Mountain Code.

I have realized that these "rules of conduct" are close to a set of guidelines for leadership. Here they are, adapted for leaders:

Be prepared

Train and be conscious. Take on leadership tasks and BE a leader as often as you can to gain experience. Pay attention to the next generation. Support any students taking on leadership tasks.

Leave word of your route

Tell those involved where you are going – publish your goals and make sure you get feedback. Keep your team informed about what's going on outside AND keep them informed about what you're up to.

Be weather-wise

Get as much intelligence as possible about what's going on in your group. Gather information and use it. Don't walk blindly into storms. Manage your stakeholders.

Be equipped for bad weather and frost

"Plan for success – prepare for disaster." Make sure you have a Plan B if necessary.

Learn from the locals

Listen to experience, but don't listen to the "nay-sayers".

Use map and compass

If there is a process that's effective and efficient, use it. If not, create it. Make sure it's understood and implemented.

Don't go solo

Probably the toughest to follow: "Great leaders don't do it alone". Ask for help. Let others impress you.

Turn back in time; sensible retreat is no disgrace

Know when to quit. Pick your fights. Good advice, but unfortunately often neglected.

Conserve energy and build a snow shelter if necessary

I don't know about snow shelters in the work place ;-), but make sure you have a sensible balance between work and the rest of your life. You will NOT be thanked if you burn yourself out.

Good luck on your leadership journey, Bon voyage or "God tur".

The Golden Castle and Trolls

I coach leaders all the time. It is amazing how many are suffering from "impostor syndrome". If you believe that one day you will be "found out" or "seen as a fraud", you are not alone. Some studies show that up to 70% of high-level leaders are afraid of being exposed as a fraud! This is the negative chatter, the internal critic that we need to manage. Sometimes I call this negative chatter the Troll.

There is a Golden Castle – way up in the mountains. It's where your dreams live. It's far away and you may only get a glimpse of it – but you know it's there.

BUT

There are Trolls in the way. Trolls are as old as the landscape they live in and they know everything about it. They live inside the mountain and they are there to stop you from getting to your Golden Castle.

There are BIG TROLLS and small trolls. The trolls are one-eyed - and they are stubborn.

They hate CHANGE, and they use all they can and all they know – not to create possibilities, but to limit your choices, and to STOP you.

How to tame the trolls?

They hate us laughing at them and cannot stand the sunlight. When they are hit by sunlight, they turn into rock and lose their power. So get them out into the sun and have a good laugh at them.

I think we all have trolls inside us. They are stubborn and one-eyed and they hate change. They know our fears and all our weaknesses and they stop us from going for our dreams. They hold us back and they make us feel like imposters. But they can be managed.

Get help, read "Taming Your Gremlins" by R.D.Carson, get a coach. Whatever you do, learn to tame your Troll!

Learning steps

Being a leader means that you must deal with change. There are changes being presented by your management, demands for change from customers or suppliers, your people need to change or learn new skills and you, yourself, need to grow and change.

One of the problems is that when we set out to change, we have to do something that we are not good at, and therefore we make mistakes and that hurts.

I don't like to fail and it gets in my way of learning new skills.

In order to learn, we must be conscious about our actions.

The following model always works when you are learning a new skill – or getting better at an existing skill. It works fine for what I am writing about: leadership skills.

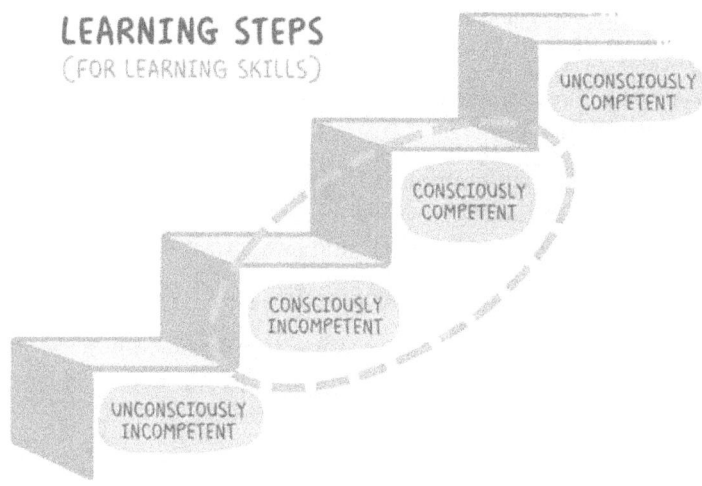

LEARNING STEPS
(FOR LEARNING SKILLS)

UNCONSCIOUSLY COMPETENT

CONSCIOUSLY COMPETENT

CONSCIOUSLY INCOMPETENT

UNCONSCIOUSLY INCOMPETENT

Let's use an example (driving a car):

When you are a child, you don't know that you don't know how to drive a car. Someone puts you in the back seat, something happens outside the windows, and some time later, you arrive at the destination. (You are unconsciously incompetent.)

When you become a late teenager, you sit in the driver's seat with an adult next to you and you very quickly become aware that you don't know how to drive a car. You learn to hate the sound of ill-timed gear changes and a stalling engine. (You are now consciously incompetent.)

After some training, you get better at it. You can do three-point turns and change gear smoothly and even drive on the motorway and you know that you know how to drive a car. You get your driving licence, but if you're honest, you still have to think about the driving. Sometimes you get lost, because you were so busy concentrating on driving safely that your brain didn't have the capacity to navigate at the same time;-) (You are now consciously competent.)

After a while, this happens: You get in the car outside your home and the next thing you know, you're in the car park at work, with no recollection of how you got there. You didn't think about the driving at all - you can drive a car without being conscious of the individual actions you needed to perform. (You are unconsciously competent.)

This model works for skill learning. You can replace driving with playing a musical instrument, listening skills, juggling three balls, presenting skills, etc.

They all pass through the same steps. And the learning only happens in Steps 2 and 3!

This is why your handwriting probably isn't any better now than it was ten years ago, even if you've done a lot of writing since then. You haven't been conscious about learning how to write in that time.

Why is it important to know about this?

You are so competent in so many ways. But if you want to get better at something (or pick up a new skill) you have to become conscious of your incompetence. And that hurts.

To be bad at something really sucks, right? This is why it is so hard for a lot of people to learn new skills. It is just plain uncomfortable and scary to admit that they are bad at whatever it is they want to learn.

If that's how you feel and you want to give up, it's because this model works! Learn to embrace your failures. They can help you to succeed.

Imagine the toddler wanting to walk. She gets up, holds the table, tries to walk and falls. She gets up, holds the table, tries to walk and falls. She gets up, holds the table, tries to walk and falls. Over and over and over again.

She NEVER says: " Naaah, this walking stuff is for the people who know how to do it, I'll stick to crawling along on the floor."

She keeps practising because she has not learned that failing is bad.

Be gentle with yourself when you learn.

Here is the explanation for this from research in neuroscience:

To learn something new, we have to use our prefrontal cortex, which takes effort. Anything we learn creates patterns in our brain – neuropatterns. (Very simply put, new synapses are created between neurons.) Every time we do something, more synapses are created (the pattern gets stronger) and this feels good, as we don't have to use our prefrontal cortex so much to think about what we are doing. We become less conscious about it.

Say we want to learn a new way of doing something we are already good at (like driving a car on the other side of the road when we move from Europe to the UK).

Your brain screams: "This is not the way to do it!" and sends warning signals (chemicals) all over your brain and body. You probably feel stressed. Your prefrontal cortex works hard to think about how to survive in the London traffic, and slowly new synapses are created and more neuropatterns are strengthened.

So, (speaking from personal experience): after a while it feels entirely normal to drive on the left side of the road, and I sometimes notice that I have become an unconsciously competent driver in London traffic.

Don't give up, and one day you'll get to your destination without even thinking about how you got there.

Learning a new leadership skill will follow this pattern. It will feel awkward the first couple of times you try it; you may think that the old ways of doing things were easier (and "better"). You just need to persist, to commit and to keep trying, and to accept that you are not a master at it yet. It sucks, right?

Keep practising and allow yourself to be consciously incompetent – and then, little by little, consciously more competent. Then, one day you'll feel good about your new skill.

Feedback or Strokes?
- both are good – and very different

Part of our job as leaders is to give feedback, and most of the people I meet neither receive nor give as much feedback as they want. Furthermore, the feedback they do give and/or receive is not of the quality they want.

I believe that one of the problems is that we don't distinguish between "strokes" and "feedback" – and we don't know HOW to give and receive feedback effectively.

Here is how I distinguish between feedback and strokes (and assessments):

- *Strokes* are "pats on the back", high-fives, saying "great job", cheering and generally just creating positivity. Train yourself to give more of these, if you need to.
- *Feedback* is a reaction or response to behaviour or an action that conveys useful information. The receiver chooses how to use the feedback.
- *Assessment* is an evaluation of HOW GOOD (or not) the performance was, usually compared to someone else's performance.

Here are some points to improve the feedback culture in your team:

- Know the difference between strokes and feedback (and assessment) – they are all important!
- Separate assessments from feedback - keep feedback factual and give it as close to the action as possible
- Demand feedback yourself
- Ask for permission to give feedback OR wait until you are asked for it.

Most people want to hear that they do a good job, they want to be cheered on, they want to hear "Great job", "Hurrah", "That was an awesome slam dunk". It makes us feel good and it increases positivity in the team. These are strokes and I believe we should give more of them. It's just not feedback.

Sometimes you are asked to assess people's performance. It can be part of the performance evaluation cycle in your company. It can be combined with feedback and strokes, but I believe it is different from both.

Let us look at an example:

You hire a trainer to improve your driving on icy roads. You go to a track and your car slides in the first left turn and goes off the tarmac. One of the following happens:

1. The trainer says: "No, no Frode, that was not good, I saw you panic there - you have to keep the back of the car from sliding". This is not useful (and it is not feedback).
2. The trainer says: "When you came into the curve, you kept turning the steering wheel to the left. This caused the car's rear wheels to slide out. I suggest that you turn the steering wheel to the right (against the turn) if you notice that the car is slipping". This is useful feedback.

Why is the second example more useful?

*   There were no assessments
*   There was no need to defend: "No, I wasn't panicking!"
*   The feedback was based on observation only and not on interpretations: "kept turning the steering wheel" vs. "saw you panic"
*   It gives a clear description of the effect of what you did: "the car's rear wheels slid…"
*   It provides a clear suggestion in a format that is actionable: "When <this happens> then <do this>"

So now you can start training yourself to give better feedback, and at the same time ask your people how you are doing (when giving feedback). You will then improve your feedback-giving skills.

One reason why it is so hard to create a feedback culture is that when someone wants to give you feedback, your limbic system will most likely have a threat or fear reaction, making it hard for you to receive the feedback.

Neuroscience tells us that our brain, when it receives a stimulus, is five times more likely to react as though it was a threat than a neutral or positive event.

So when you tell someone: "I want to give you some feedback", he will most likely have a negative reaction. Look at the Be SAFE &

Certain model, and work out for yourself how many ways this person might feel threatened by your offer!

IF the feedback is:

- requested by the person
- given right after the experience
- specific and concrete enough to help the person change some behaviour next time
- given in a tone and a setting that shows the person that you want to support him and NOT evaluate

THEN it might be useful.

Good leaders accept feedback, great leaders demand feedback.

Do you REALLY want to get better?

Something has to be at stake.

What does it mean to have something at stake? My interpretation is that something is VERY IMPORTANT for you or you are COMMITTED to something.

Let us say you want to get better at something. Some examples might be to: give better feedback, get better at delegating, improve your handwriting, run a marathon in under four hours, get better at tennis or playing the piano.

How are you going to keep up the training during the uncomfortable phase when you are consciously incompetent? It sucks to be really bad at something, and that's when most people quit.

You need to have an internal or external commitment. It has to be important for you. Something has to be at stake. And you have to be conscious about your training.

If the commitment is internal, promise yourself to train every day. Help yourself by acknowledging it, something like: "If I practise this for at least half an hour every day this month, I will improve". Put up a list of dates and tick off the days you do it. Give yourself praise. Admit that it is hard and tap into your ability to be disciplined.

Some of us like to have external commitments. We tell a friend we're going to train and arrange to check in with him or her about our progress. We enter a marathon, maybe invite sponsorship, and that can make us feel committed to train and improve. Maybe you join a small group of musicians and you want to improve your piano playing before you perform in public.

Here is my personal example: I noticed one day that I sometimes used bad language at work. I swore. Not so often that people had complained, but I was uncomfortable with it. It was a bad habit I wanted to get rid off. At the next departmental meeting, I made a bet with everyone: "If you catch me swearing in the next three months, I will put 50 kroner (about £5) in the summer-party collection box."

Here is what happened: My consciousness was very high, because some of my friends tried constantly to trick me into swearing, and I got rid of a bad habit. It cost me £15.

This was, of course, not about the money, but about commitment and consciousness. It was important enough for me to stay conscious about my language.

Something was at stake.

Practice doesn't make perfect.

We often hear that "practice makes perfect". Well, I don't think so. Look at your handwriting. You've had a lot of practice, right? Is it better than it was ten years ago?

Another example is your driving skills. Be really honest: are you a better driver now than you were ten years ago? If so, you've probably been training.

If you want to get better at something, sure you have to do it a lot, but just *doing* isn't enough. Only if you *train* will you get better. My definition of training is that you have consciousness about what you are doing and you get feedback upon which you act. Then you'll actually improve your skills.

Here are a few ways you can raise your consciousness about what you are training in:

- Get support. Involve some people you trust in your plan to improve and ask them to give you straight feedback.
- Make the video camera your coach. The camera doesn't lie. I know it's awkward in the beginning to video yourself - and your voice sounds funny ;-) - but if you are serious about improving, it's very effective.
- Take notes. Journal. Reflect. Think through what worked and what didn't work - let go of what didn't work and do more of what worked.

So let's say you want to get better at giving clear, concise and compelling messages. After each message you deliver, ask some of the recipients:

What did you like about it? How can I improve?

Don't settle for "Yes, Frode, it was OK and I liked it". Ask them to be as specific as possible. What worked? What didn't work? What would have given it more impact / meaning / clarity?

Train, don't practise.

Representatives

The medieval "fool" is currently misunderstood by many. Nowadays he (usually a he) is seen as a funny figure with a funny hat who made jokes and made people laugh. Yup, that was also his role, but a more important role of the fool was that he could tell the King the truth without having his head chopped off. The King knew that the court mostly told him what they thought he wanted to hear. I believe that a lot of the corporate "kings" today should hire a corporate fool.

Yes, I know that today we have something called the ombudsman, one of the (few) words that the Norwegian language has given the world. The ombudsman's job is to deal with organisational issues and complaints, but the corporate fool is in closer relationship with the boss.

Whenever I was "the boss" it made my life easier if the people working for me had "representatives". And I truly believe it made their life easier, too.

During good times and bad times, there are occasions when the information flow is difficult. Sometimes there are tough decisions to be made (or communicated) and sometimes you (as the boss) need to hear something that is hard for a single person to tell you.

I have found it very useful to utilize the representative.

Some of you work in industries or organizations where this is business as usual – you have union reps or someone in a similar role. If you don't, encourage your people to have a representative. That person can deliver messages for the group and cannot be "punished" for speaking up.

I truly believe in Deep Democracy and processes where all voices can be heard – but unfortunately, sometimes the hierarchy is such that some people will not speak their minds in front of the boss. However, they may have the courage to give the message through the representative.

He or she doesn't have to wear a funny hat, but seriously, there was a time when I was hired by a CEO to be "the corporate fool". When he hired me, he said: *"Great, now I get to know everything that's happening in the organisation. You will be there and watch and listen and tell me what's going on"*. My answer was: *"No, sir, but you will get to know more about yourself"*.

This CEO learned a lot about himself, his impact and how to improve the relationship with the people in that organisation. He also learned about some issues that otherwise would not have surfaced, and which could potentially have created serious conflicts if not dealt with.

Problems cannot be solved

A long time ago I attended my very first leadership training program. Here I met a wise old man (he was probably about the age I am now). He taught me a sentence that I have tried to live by ever since:

"Only worry about something once."

At the time, I didn't quite get what it meant, but later I put it in the context of problems, boundary conditions and challenges and then it made perfect sense.

Some years ago, someone decided that we shouldn't talk about problems. It was better to call them challenges. So everybody just swapped these words, and from then on, problems were called challenges. Big deal.

I believe there is another way of looking at this:

- A PROBLEM is a statement about something that you think is wrong: "The machine at line 3 is broken". "I have two flat tyres on my car." These cannot be solved.
- A CHALLENGE is formulated in a sentence that starts with "How to…" or "How do I…":
  "How to fix the machine on line 3." "How to fix two flat tyres when you only have one spare wheel." This opens possibilities to look for solutions.
- A BOUNDARY CONDITION is something that you accept and stop worrying about.
  "It rains a lot in my home town."

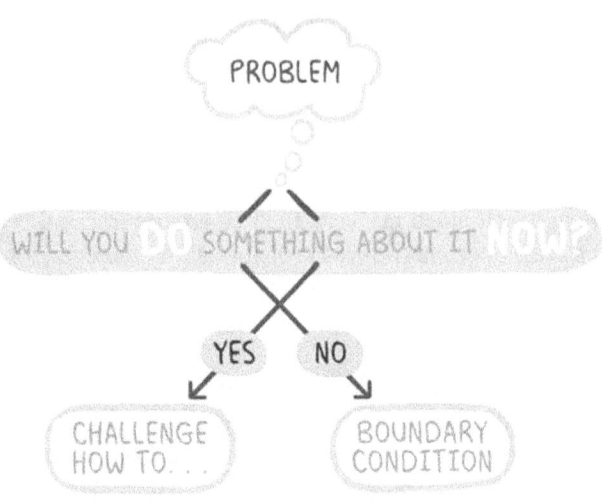

The figure shows the relationship between these aspects.

If someone states something that sounds like a problem, ask the question: "Will you do something about it NOW?"

If yes, then formulate a How to-sentence.

If no, it is a boundary condition.

The answer to the question can change over time. (Tomorrow you will decide to do something about it).

Example 1:

It rains a lot in my home town.

Will I do something about it now?

No – it's a boundary condition.

OR

It rains a lot in my home town and I get wet on my way to work.

Will I do something about it now?

Yes – Challenge: "How to get to work without getting wet?"

Lots of possibilities.

Example 2:

One Monday morning there are two flat tyres on my car.

Will I do something about it NOW?

No – it just IS.

So what is the challenge NOW?

"How to get to work."

Lots of possibilities.

When my colleagues hear about this, they keep asking: "Aren't you worried about the two flat tyres?"

"No, I'll worry about that on Saturday; right now it's a boundary condition. On Saturday morning, I'll make it a challenge: "How to fix two flat tyres when I only have one spare".

Lots of possibilities.

Train yourself on your problems, challenges and boundary conditions.

Here's the challenge in most peoples' lives: How to stop worrying about boundary conditions.

As you saw above, when you worry about something, it should only be when you answer the question "Will I do something about it NOW?" with a YES, and then find the solution to the Challenge. NOT when you accept Boundary Conditions.

P2S C2P
- getting rid of the monkey

A long time ago, Harvard Business Review wrote the story about the monkeys. The exact wording of the story isn't important, but it is about the person walking up to you with a monkey on the shoulder, and when the person leaves, YOU have the monkey sitting on YOUR shoulder.

The monkey is, of course, the problems that other people bring to you.

Here's an attempt in making you a monkey-free zone.

This will challenge your belief in what makes you worthy of your salary.

First let's talk about the new leader's dilemma: You get hired as an expert and you are given A LOT of positive feedback (and promotion!) because you solve problems. So you seek out problems to solve. And it gives you a great feeling to solve them. You LOVE problems. And you are seen - and see yourself - as someone who is GOOD at solving problems. And it gives you a sense of worth.

When someone approaches you with a problem (or challenge) you feel very good when you can solve it for him or her.

Occasionally you need some time to solve it, the person leaves and you are stuck with the monkey. After this happens a few times, your space looks like a zoo – you have all the monkeys.

The dilemma? This is not leadership. Leaders don't solve everbody else's problems, they support them in selecting SOLUTIONS.

You can decide TODAY that you will live after the following simple rule:

P2S
Problem - 2 - Solutions

IF someone comes to you with a Problem, THEN expect him or her to come with at least two possible Solutions.

The rationale is that if someone has seen the problem, that person is closer to the solutions.

Dare to trust this:

The reason you have people reporting to you IS NOT that you're there to solve their problems, but to support them in getting the job done. And to help them select the best solution.

"If you give a person a fish, you feed her for a day. If you teach a person to fish, you feed her for life."

While you are at it, add this rule also (it really is just another version of P2S):

C2P
Complaints - 2 - Proposals

We all know people who whine and complain that "the food is too bland", "the parking space is too far away", "the carpets are too dark", "the coffee is too cold", etc etc.

Help them by implementing the following rule. "In our group, we have this rule: If you are going to complain, come up with at least two proposals for what you are going to DO about it".

One out of two outcomes will happen: Either these people will start thinking more positively and finding solutions (that's good). Or they will stop complaining (that's also good).

The fear of disappointment

It's a vicious circle. We want people to have the courage to take more risks, to act courageously, and yet they don't.

One reason people are afraid of taking risks is that they are afraid of failing. Our limbic system tries to keep us feeling safe and protected: "Don't do it. You may fail, and you will be disappointed and your friends (boss, colleagues) will stop wanting to be with you. You will end up lonely and sad."

This is a truly vicious circle.

What is needed? I believe we must change two things. The system (boss, colleagues, organization and team) must get better at celebrating failure. We must create conversations where you get credit for having tried, for having shown courage, for choosing to act in the right way, even if the outcome wasn't what we wanted.

AND we must work on our own ability to be with failure and disappointment. Through most of your training, feedback and education, you have succeeded, so you are probably not very OK with being disappointed. Your brain (the limbic system) will do its best to protect you. It will hold you back from taking any risk where there is even a small chance of failing, because it will convince you that it is better to make sure you are not disappointed.

Both of these changes start with awareness of what is going on. If you understand that the lack of risk-taking is connected to the fear of failure and the subsequent fear of disappointment, then you can do something about it. You can start a conversation in your team – "How do we deal with failure around here?" AND you can look at yourself and keep developing your ability to "be with" failure and disappointment.

Getting outside help – a coach, a team coach or a facilitator - may be the fastest way of speeding up the process towards more risk-taking.

What really happens is, of course, neuro-biology: We do what we are good at and the brain gives its receptors doses of dopamine to feel good about this behaviour.

Then we want something to change – we need to do something we are NOT good at. The brain sees the threat and issues "red alert" drugs and we feel the threat and the fear.

The prefrontal cortex tries to make sense of this and interprets it as "fear of failing". It then come up with all kinds of reasonable excuses as to why we shouldn't do this at all.

Your job is to develop stars

You are not responsible for your people's continuous development. Your job is to make them realize that they themselves are completely responsible to update themselves, to seek more education and to attend the courses that are appropriate.

Here's why – this is the story you must get your people to understand:

When you end your education, you have a high degree of freedom and you have a (relatively) high degree of capability – you are a star. You can afford to take risks in your career.

Then you start taking on responsibilities in your life – spouse, house and kids, mortgage, cars and stuff that are all OK, but that lower your degree of freedom.

AND the world changes, so your (relative) capability drops.

If you let both of these happen – and you don't do anything about them - you will end up in the "quadrant of humiliation" in the diagram below – where you have to take anything from the boss, because you are afraid of losing your job.

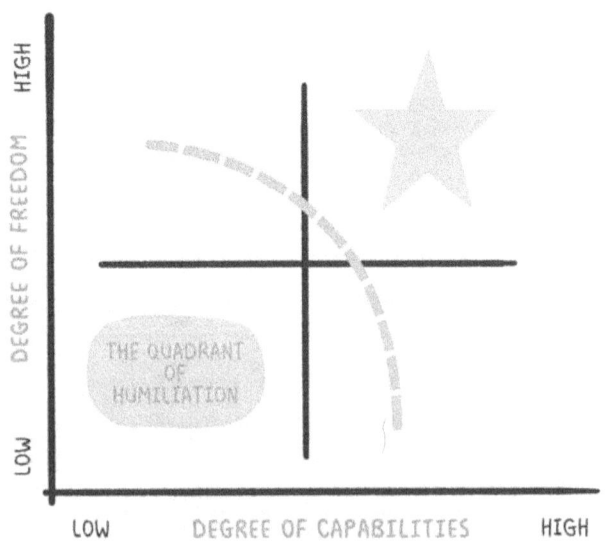

It is OK if you want to be a surfer dude and have all the freedom in the world – then capabilities may not be not so important - OR if you want to be the world's most capable (of whatever you are) – then it is maybe not so important to have a large degree of freedom.

For most of us – we have to make sure we stay above the curved line in the figure. We must have enough freedom and be sufficiently capable that we're not afraid of taking risks and failing.

The best, of course, is to be a star, but for most of us: STAY ABOVE THE CURVED LINE.

Please have all your people (and yourself!) understand this diagram.

If you trust that your boss is going to take care of you and develop you and make sure that you grow your capabilities: SORRY! Chances are, that boss won't be around when you wake up one morning and find yourself in "the quadrant of humiliation".

Delegation
- a five step program

Gerard M. Blair of the University of Edinburgh says, "Delegation is a skill of which we have all heard – but which few understand. It can be used either as an excuse for dumping failure onto the shoulders of subordinates, or as a dynamic tool for motivating and training your team to realize their full potential".

I often hear leaders say they want to be better at delegation. When I ask them what exactly it is that they want to get better at – what skill they want to improve – they don't know or they answer "delegation".

It makes your life easier if you look at delegation as a five-step process. Each step requires different skills or understanding:

1. You have to know what it is you want to delegate (What is the task?)
2. You have to know who to delegate to (Who can do the job?)
3. You have to dare to let go of the task (Do I trust anyone else to do this?)
4. You have to be able to specify what your expected result is (What is the product?)
5. You have to ensure that the result is acceptable afterwards (Is this good enough?)

Most leaders have different challenges with one or more of these steps. In the following I'll address each one of them.

1. Knowing what to delegate

Let's look at the first step of Delegation: what you can or cannot delegate.

You cannot delegate the accountability for the task. Accountability stays with you, but you can delegate the responsibility and authority to do the job.

You cannot delegate personnel tasks like motivation, praising, reprimanding, performance reviews and promotion.

Look at the tasks that you did before you got promoted. These are probably the easiest to delegate, since you know that people in your former job (you) were able to do them. And you know how to describe the job.

Look for tasks that will motivate the people doing them. Look for decisions that can be taken by someone other than you. Yes, it is possible (and recommended) to delegate decisions.

Make sure you empower the person with enough authority to actually do the job his or her way.

Simple example:

Telling someone to check all printers for ink every Friday will ensure that every printer is checked every Friday.

Delegating to someone the task of making sure the printers don't run out of ink will enable this person to find a way to make sure that the printers are filled up when they need ink.

Look for opportunities to delegate tasks that will develop the person. If you give someone a "wow" task that they may get overwhelmed by – make sure you support them and let them take over gradually.

Look carefully at the "boring" tasks that you feel are easy to delegate. Distribute them evenly in your group and then sprinkle the exciting tasks around. Talk to your people about what they want. You may be surprised about who wants to do what. You really want to use this to motivate your people.

Look for more opportunities to delegate. Look at the tasks you are doing. Do you have to do them? Would it be possible for someone else to do some of them? If you delegate more, you will be able to spend more time leading and coaching your people.

Imagine how much more time you'll have if, when a new task lands on your desk, you always ask: "Who else can do this?"

2. Who do you delegate to?

Okay, so you have chosen the task to delegate. Now, let us look at who else can do the job.

How do you know? What do you really know about your people? How do you know what they want?

When I started out wanting to get better at delegation, I focused almost entirely on the tasks and what I wanted done, and then I looked at how busy my people were and I set up an agreement with them: "I'll keep pushing jobs at you and you have the responsibility to tell me NO when it's too much".

It wasn't enough. I had forgotten (or really, not learned) that our people should be part of the delegation process. So talk to them. Present the tasks at hand and learn from them what they can and want to do. No, it is not a democracy, but it can be a process where you learn about their capabilities and what motivates them.

Look for tasks that will stretch them. Look for examples where you are still doing a task because you used to do it before your promotion: who is doing your 'old' job now? Can she (with some coaching, support and follow-up) take on that task?

This part of the delegation process is about having great conversations with your people about what is possible beyond the tasks they are currently doing.

3. Do I dare to delegate?

The first two parts of the delegation process are relatively easy. Now it gets tougher.

One of my clients inspired me to write about delegation.

Jimmy said: "You see, Frode, I know how to delegate, how to find the tasks and match them to the people that can grow from them. But I still don't do it."

"Why not?"

"Because I believe that I am assessed and judged by what I deliver. If I stop being the expert and the doer, I will lose my power and my credibility and I don't dare to risk that."

Right!

So how can I help you understand that a leader is NOT the doer? By writing about P2S and the monkeys? By asking you to take a good look at your own beliefs and to challenge them?

This fear of leading and delegating is absolutely normal, especially in relatively new leaders.

You have been given all kinds of positive feedback on all the good stuff you have delivered. You were probably originally hired as an expert. Everybody came (and still comes) to you for answers and for the good stuff that you are so quick in delivering.

And now you are going to tell them that someone else is going to deliver? With a potentially lower quality and it's going to take longer?

YES.

This is one of the tougher choices you have to make. It is why I say leadership is a CHOICE. Only when you choose to delegate will the knowledge about how and to whom to delegate be useful.

Only when you trust that you will be assessed by your peers, people and your boss on your leadership skills and by how your team is performing, only then will this work.

Yes, I do know that part of your job IS to deliver and your boss also expects this from you. Life isn't always easy. Know the difference between a boundary condition, a challenge and a problem, and challenge yourself to delegate what you can. Start small and keep training.

I wish you strength and courage.

4. How do I tell them what I want?

So you have figured out what and to whom to delegate – and you have overcome your fear of actually doing it. How do you deliver the message?

Explain as best you can what you want and continue by having a conversation with the receiver:

- What is her understanding of the task?
- What does she need in order to do the task?
- What is the expectation YOU have for the result, and how will you both know when it is good enough?
- When do you expect delivery?
- Are the targets SMART (if applicable?)

If you are delegating a decision or a responsibility – continue the discussion about the boundaries.

Stay out of too much detail on HOW to do the job, but be available for coaching and support if needed.

Agree on checkpoints and milestones.

And then: Let her get on with it.

Yep, it's back to the daring-to-let-go-discussion. Stay off.

5. How do I accept the result?

After you have done all the good work of Delegation, there comes a moment which is NOT easy. Anna comes to you with the result and you have to evaluate it. You have probably noticed that the result is NOT exactly what it would have been had you done it yourself.

This is a very important leadership moment. You have to make a choice. Is it good enough?

Why did you delegate in the first place? Look again at the quote on page 105 "Delegation ... can be used ... as a dynamic tool for motivating and training your team..."

Instead of asking what is wrong with the result, have a conversation with Anna. Look at what went well. Discuss what could be improved. Give suggestions. (If you don't have suggestions, does that show that you couldn't do it better yourself?)

Is it completely unacceptable? Why? What went wrong in the whole process? There are four preceding steps. Were all of them perfectly executed from your side?

This is team work. Learn to love having the conversations with your team on how to become better. There is always an improvement to be made next time.

I'll quote my friend Endre:

"I remember a story about a Japanese manager who was given an important report by his employee. After reading the report, he looked at his employee, smiled, and said: "This is very good. Now let's see if we can make it even better."

This is a very different approach with a very different outcome. This approach shows respect for the person and the work that has been done, it creates a joint responsibility for making it even better, and it potentially creates energy around improvement."

Section 4
Making your day job easier

I heard it first from Kåre Willoch, an old Norwegian statesman: "Really, we should all have our grandchildren first".

So maybe it is possible to learn from others.

When I worked as a management consultant, I studied management tools and realized that once you started practising them, you added your own flavour to them, or you found some interesting way to improve on them. The following are some of these add-ons.

.

Process development tool

It's really part of everyone's job, in an organisation, to make sure that the processes are as effective as possible. So you may be involved in process development work. Through this project there may be experts and software available to help you. Nevertheless, the following is a tip that I have found very useful when it comes to drawing / illustrating the process:

Make sure your process is mapped horizontally with the stakeholders (or whoever is responsible for the activity/task) named down the side. (See figure below).

It will make your life easier in many ways.

The process map becomes easier to read.

And the crossing of lines from one department to another becomes very visible. In your process development you want to have as few of these as possible. They create overheads, bottlenecks and misunderstandings.

An efficient process usually looks good on paper too, with a minimum of mess and lines crossing and going up and down etc.

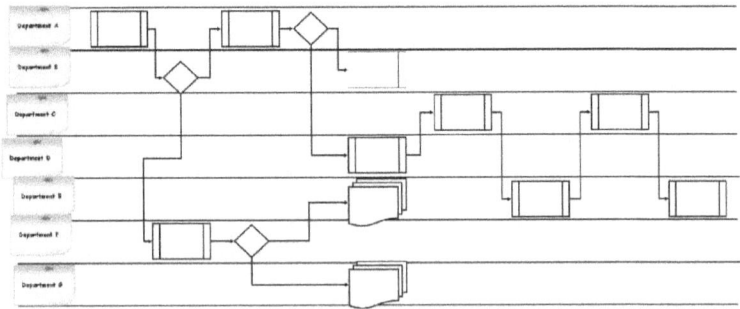

Stakeholders

A friend of mine was hired by a somewhat old-fashioned entertainment house with a dwindling audience and not very interesting artists (or vice versa). Her job was to book "fresher" artists. The owners were in the process of expanding, and would, in the near future, have more scenes, more gigs and needed a younger audience. Anna did a great job. She had a lot of contacts in the entertainment circuit, the company pulled bigger crowds than in years, and she felt great.

One day the marketing manager took her aside and said that since they had now decided to book all artists through an impresario, she wasn't needed any more.

My friend was totally taken by surprise.

I really feel bad for the first time leaders I have met in my career who seem to think that if they only do their job well, they will succeed and be recognized and their projects will run smoothly.

When we hear the term "office politics", many of us have a negative feeling about it. It seems to imply smooching the bosses and greasing the way for your project.

Some of us like the term "stakeholder management" better.

I think they mean the same thing; it's up to you to choose your own perspective.

Stakeholder management is important because it's the stakeholders around you who determine whether or not you are going to be successful. You are NOT in this alone.

So who are the stakeholders? There are probably far more of them than you originally thought.

This is what you need to do to manage your stakeholders:

1. Identify them. Do not do this alone. Involve your team, your boss, your peers, your customers and others (who are, of course, all stakeholders themselves). Put your job/project in focus and keep scanning around you. Who can have, or will

have, an INTEREST or an INFLUENCE on your job/project? List them as best you can - use personal names, not department names or organizations.

2. Sort them. Hopefully, you now realize that there are a lot of stakeholders. We don't want to work harder; we want to work smarter, so we have to give the different kinds of stakeholders different kinds of attention. One way of sorting them is by Influence and Interest. See the diagram below.

STAKEHOLDER SORTING MATRIX

- The easy ones are the "A"s. They are easily identified and they show themselves.
- Look out for "B"s. They don't easily show themselves, but they may stop your efforts and your project.
- Manage the "C"s – they may not have too much influence today, but they may one day move to "B" or "A".
- Decide what to do about the "D"s.

Now, make a plan. For EACH stakeholder you have to know:

- What you want from her or what you want her to do?
- What does the stakeholder want?
- How do you (or your team) relate to each stakeholder in a way that creates a win-win?

What my friend didn't do was look to see who had any influence on her success. She believed that as long as she booked the right artists and got bigger audiences she would be fine. Not so. She forgot to stay in touch with the marketing people and the people who wanted simpler contracts (all handled through one channel) and the owners who were surprised to see that the new artists were more expensive than the old ones.

"The cycle"

The cycle I'm talking about here is the yearly cycle: You set out in the beginning by creating targets or goals for your people. You coach your people and follow up their progress during the year and then – at the request of HR(?) – you assess them.

Some of us take over a team in the middle of the cycle, so we have to assess our people based on targets and goals that were set before we entered the scene. By the previous boss. Not fun.

Some of us have experienced how hard it is to set SMART targets. Maybe we don't do a very good job with them and then we REALLY regret that, when the time comes to evaluate performance towards them.

Some of us have a hard time evaluating other peoples' performance.

The following are some things I wish I'd known when I started out.

How to be SMART

Ok, so you have decided to create SMART targets for your people. Like many other great acronyms, SMART has multiple definitions:

S - Specific, significant, stretching
M - Measurable, meaningful, motivational
A - Agreed upon, attainable, achievable, acceptable, action-oriented
R - Realistic, relevant, reasonable, rewarding, results-oriented
T - Time-based, timely, tangible, trackable

All of these words are useful and I'm sure we have all learned them somewhere, and yet it is STILL difficult to assess performance afterwards, right?

Here's a useful way to look at SMART targets. When you start the cycle and set out to create targets, make sure you talk with your people, starting with some simple questions:

- How will we know if you have achieved these targets?
- What will it look like to achieve them 50%?
- What will it mean to overachieve?

- What does it MEAN "to get better at...?

Create some examples, record them and bring them back at the end of the period.

You must have this discussion at the outset. Most assessment conversations go bad because we don't have a useful way of agreeing what the achievement IS when we are in the assessment itself and the person's promotion/salary increase etc is on the line.

This is like an investment – the real benefit will be seen at the end of the period.

The good news: You will get better at this. When you've had some really tricky assessment conversations where you couldn't agree on how to measure the achievements, you will willingly learn how to do a better job by setting SMART targets and AGREEING how to measure them at the start of the cycle.

Assessments – judging your people

When I started out as a leader, one of the hardest parts of my job (I thought) was to assess my people. I worked in an oil-company and once or twice a year the HR department rolled out the performance evaluation process. I had to grade people, and rank them. I felt bad about evaluating my people; I thought they were all good. And anyway, how was I going to be able to judge their performance?

If this sounds familiar, let's look at how to change your perspective on your situation.

Imagine an athlete who is training. And training. And is getting better but never gets to compete. What will happen to his motivation?

Everyone wants to be good at something and everybody wants to know how good they are compared to others. (If this is NOT true for someone in your team, you might want to have a different conversation with him or her.)

For now, let's assume it's correct. Then you owe it to your people to help them evaluate how good they are.

It is a circle. You start the process by agreeing on clear targets, SMART goals and how to achieve them. You coach them during the period (year), and at the end of the period (year), you evaluate their performance in relation to the goals and targets. And then you can start again with new targets and goals. The cycle continues year after year.

At a particular point in the cycle you are NOT the coach or the friend or the colleague. You are the representative of the company. You are the boss. You are actually there to judge the performance. To tell them how good they are. And to tell them what needs to improve.

Make sure you are factual, that your assessment is based on facts and figures. This is the hardest part if you initially created targets and goals that were not SMART and can't readily be evaluated now. Hopefully, you made sure the targets were SMART in the first place. Make sure you listen to their point of view and get their input on how they evaluate their work towards the goals and targets. Maybe your assessment isn't too far from their own?

Now, you may work in a company that has a system or process for performance management. That could be useful here.

However, nowadays, as we understand more and more about how our brains work, many companies seems to realize that performance management processes just don't give us what we want from them.

So you may have other forms of processes run by HR. My point here is that most people I have met want to know how they are doing. They crave feedback. It may not be in the form of grades or bonus schemes etc, but your people deserve that you give them feedback on how they are in relation to the plans / goals you agreed.

Important vs Urgent

One way of looking at leadership: It is about doing what is important, avoiding the things that are not important, managing crises and delegating what others can do for us.

How much of your time do you spend on tasks that are URGENT, but not IMPORTANT? (By "important" I mean important for *you* to do.)

How much time do you have left to spend on tasks that really *are* IMPORTANT? They may not be urgent at all! (These are usually the leadership tasks like planning and prevention, reflecting, developing your people, building relationships, exercising, etc.)

And how many of these IMPORTANT tasks do you just not get round to doing because they are not urgent?

The matrix below can help you sort all your tasks into four quadrants according to Importance and Urgency. Ask yourself what is really important for you to do yourself. What is not important? What is urgent and what is not urgent? Keep doing this on a regular basis. Include your team.

Then ask yourself: Do I really want to waste time on tasks that are not important?

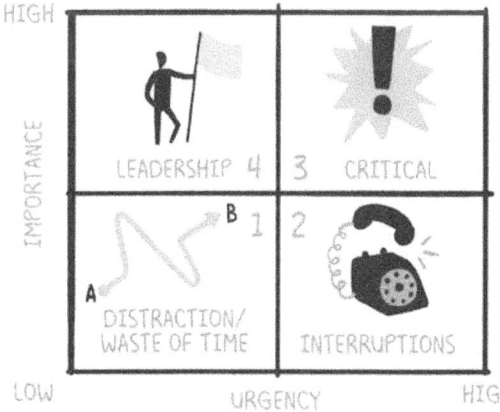

Here's a way of dealing with the tasks in each quadrant:

1. **Avoid these**
   Tell those around you that these will not be done. Only when NO OTHER tasks need attention will these be addressed. These are the distractions like reading emails every five minutes, etc.

2. **Delegate these**
   It is not important that you do these yourself but they could be important for others to learn from. Note: These may seem important, but they just have imminent deadlines. Lots of stuff that is fun and easy to do belongs here.

3. **Manage these**
   If your life consists mostly of tasks that are urgent and important, you should seek help in prioritizing AND looking at the goals of your job.

4. **Spend more time here**
   Take more time to plan, reflect, prevent, build your team and carry out other tasks that are important – but not urgent.

Make this quadrant public – discuss it with your team, update it regularly and spend time on what's important.

Bathtubs

What does a bathtub have to do with training?

Imagine that you have a bathtub almost full of cold water and that you want to heat it up. One way of doing it is to take a small cup, fill it with cold water from the tub, bring it over a heater, wait a couple of minutes until the water is hot, and pour it back into the water. Then wait a little, refill the cup from the tub and repeat.

Not a very effective process.

The water in the bathtub may never heat up.

So what has this got to do with training? You've probably guessed. A lot of organizations send their leaders off on a management / leadership course, but when the leaders come back, they have no support and the changes that they wanted to implement just don't happen. And the people surrounding the leader don't always help, making statements like: "Yeah, yeah – the boss has been on that course. Let's just ignore his attempts to change things for a couple of weeks; he'll be back to normal soon."

We tend to fill the bathtub (the organization we want to change) with tiny little changes (leaders sent on leadership course), with very little effect.

You may not be in charge of your company's training policies and you may be happy to get out of the office occasionally to "be heated up" on a training course. Just know that the change that you want in your team or department may not be implemented, since the team was not trained together.

You may have heard the saying "Culture eats strategy for breakfast". An example is when you come back from a training course and want to implement changes. Your team has NOT been on the training, they have their culture (ways of doing things) and change is hard. You have not been given enough opportunities to practise your new skills, so you may feel awkward when trying them on your team, and then stop.

It does not have to be this way. If you really want to implement change in your team, talk about it with your team, and insist that your team train together. Bring the trainers in-house or read the literature together. Implement the changes in your team. Involve your team in your development as a leader. Present this metaphorical bathtub story to the people making decisions about leadership training in your organisation.

Meetings - planning, conducting and afterwards

Mike Tyson isn't usually reckoned as a great philosopher, but I love this quote: *"Everyone has a plan – until they are punched in the mouth"*.

I have so often seen people with great plans for how to run their project, run their business, deal with their people or conduct their meeting etc. And then reality kicks in: things change and yet they stick to their original plan even if it will no longer take them towards their goal.

So: "Plan for success and prepare for disaster". Don't forget that it is the skills and the abilities of your people that will ultimately get you to the goal. The plan is temporary, and only one way of getting to the goal. Keep the goal in sight and be prepared to change everything in order to achieve it.

Let's look at the purpose and agenda of a meeting.

Bill, a friend of mine, shared this story:

Bill was invited to a series of meetings with high-ranking government folks, led by a guy named Stuart. They were just getting started in the first meeting when Tony, one of the others, politely interrupted the chairman and said: "Stuart, just one question before we dive in. What do you really want us to get done here?"

Stuart was caught a bit off guard but it was obvious Tony was trying to be helpful so he answered. "Well, you have the agenda... uh...right here. We're going to talk about ..." Tony interrupted again. "Hey, no, the agenda looks great, Stuart, but what do you really want us to get accomplished before we leave? We're with you, but what do you want us to truly get done before we walk out that door?"

Stuart considered the question and came up with the couple of things he thought were the top priorities. And it helped the meeting.

The following day, another meeting; different topic, different chair. Same Tony, same question. A couple of days later, a conference call and Tony said the same thing. Each time it was helpful, but after a few meetings, what do you think people started doing, knowing that Tony would be in the meeting? They started writing the articulated goal of the meeting across the top of the agenda, and it improved the effectiveness of the group.

You can be the Tony of your group by asking his question.

So here's what I want for you: Whenever you are planning a meeting, make sure that you know its PURPOSE.

What do you want people to achieve in the meeting? What do you want them to KNOW, FEEL and DO after the meeting? Are the right people invited?

Imagine that the purpose of the meeting is the goal, like getting to the top of the mountain. The Agenda is ONE WAY of getting there, but not the only way; it needs to be flexible.

At the beginning of the meeting, clarify the goal and agenda with the group.

Conducting the meeting

Ok, so you know the purpose of the meeting, you have invited only the people who need to be there, and you have agreed on the agenda. Now what? Here are a couple of hints to make your meetings better.

Use "What I like about that..."

To create more positivity in your meetings, encourage more positive interaction. Train your people to start their sentence with "What I like about that..." before attacking or disagreeing with or – at best – building upon, what the previous speaker said.

Here are some benefits: The speaker feels listened to. The next speaker actually has to listen to be able to find something good about what was just said (or at least acknowledge the other person's view). The people in the room starts realizing that we are all working towards the same goal (or purpose) but we may have fundamentally different views on how to get there.

Train people to listen better:

Do a little exercise. One day, when sitting around with some of your colleagues, friends, family members etc, try this:

Everybody clap their hands on their knees. It makes a noise, right? Keep clapping. Listen to the noise coming from your own clapping. That's easy. Now, listen to the sound of the clapping of the person next to you. Then, listen to the sound of someone else's clapping.

Keep moving your attention around the group – and include the sound of all the hands clapping. Carry on for a while, moving your attention every few seconds.

Is it possible to listen to someone else's clapping? Of course it is. What does it take?

Willingness, focus, concentration and attention.

Most of the time when we're having a conversation, we're probably listening to the sound of our own thoughts, more interested in 'what's in my box' than in really listening to the other person.

If you want to have better conversations – leading to better relationships – you must start with listening. Put 'your box' aside for a while and concentrate on what the other person is saying.

Practise moving your attention over to the other person. Find what it takes to "put your attention over there" just like when you listened to the clapping. Now you can actively listen to the other person – listen to understand, not to argue.

You know you have been active listening when you are tired afterwards. There is a reason why it's called "active listening". It takes effort.

Be the focus of attention:

A meeting is a team effort – and you are the leader.

This does not mean that you have to do all the work. It is very hard to facilitate the meeting and at the same time capture what needs to be captured, so delegate note-taking to someone else and make sure you remain the focus of attention.

You can then concentrate on moving the meeting towards the goal.

Use the GROW model:

The GROW model is a great tool to help a group focus, solve problems or come up with solutions to challenges.

G – Goal – what do we want to get to?

R – Reality or Roadblocks – what is the current situation and what is stopping us from getting to where we want to be?

O – Options for getting around the Roadblocks

W – Willingness or Way forward

Imagine a mountain with your Goal at the top. If there were a paved road leading from where you are right now directly to the Goal, you wouldn't need a meeting. There are Roadblocks stopping you from getting there. Our job is to find Options and suggestions for overcoming the Roadblocks or obstacles. When we have found a number of solutions, we choose the one that we are Willing to do, and then implement the Way forward.

Questions that you can ask the team:

What is our goal? Let us express the goal in SMART format.

What is stopping us from getting to the goal? Let us capture these obstacles/roadblocks.

Which ones have the biggest impact?

What are some options to overcome these roadblocks? Use different techniques to sample options – brainstorming is just one method. Use "Yes, and…" to generate many ideas.

Which of these options looks most effective? Are we willing to implement it? How? By when? Who is accountable?

By the way, the GROW model is also great in one-to-one conversations, and even when you are on your own. You can search online or offline for creative ways to use the GROW model.

After the meeting

Here's a way to save time on the minutes of the meeting (MoM).

You may work in an organization where there are formal guidelines that the MoM should follow. Even so, the following may be useful.

Always – I mean ALWAYS – ask what the purpose of the meeting is. Yes, I know you have an agenda and you have spent time deciding on absolutely the shortest list of people who have to attend and you've sent out the agenda in advance and all that good stuff, and still: ALWAYS ask what the purpose of the meeting is. What is it that you want to achieve and what is going to BE DONE as a result of the meeting?

At the end of the meeting you should have a list of tasks. This goes into the left column and will be part of your RACI diagram, that we will describe in the next paragraphs.

Who is Accountable for each task or decision? By when is it going to be finished / implemented / done?

This list should be the outcome of your meeting. A simple task list that will be used to update your ongoing RACI.

Add: "The purpose of this meeting was:…" as a heading, and your assessment of whether or not this was achieved at the end of the page. Voilà, there are your Minutes of Meeting - done.

Purpose of the meeting was….

Task	☺	Timing
Task 01	John	Done 03.04
Task 02	Linda	Started 06.04
Task 03	Jimmy	1st draft 05.04
Descision 01	John	Done 05.04
…		

Comments…

RACI

Here's a simple tool to use in your department, project or any time two or more people work together. It helps agree on who's doing what.

R - Responsible or Resource

A - Accountable

C - Consulted

I - Informed

"Responsible" or "Resource" means the person having to deliver the task.

"Accountable" means ultimately responsible; the person who has this as his/her responsibility towards the outside world, or "where the buck stops".

"Consulted" – person(s) who will be asked for opinions, checked with and generally involved in decisions.

"Informed" – person(s) who must be informed of progress and decisions.

Persons / Tasks	Jenny	Jimmy	Anne	Fred	Lisa	John	
Task 1	R		I	I		A	
Task 2	I	R		C	R		
Task 3	A		R	C	R	A	
Task 4	R	A/R		C		C	
Task 5	C			I	A		
Task 6	R		A	R		C	

Sample RACI diagram

First, list all the tasks and/or responsibilities down the side of the RACI chart and all the persons involved across the top. Look for individuals, not department names or groups. Individuals.

Now, start a conversation. Go through the list of tasks and ask: "Who is accountable for this task? Who is responsible? Who must be consulted? And who needs to be informed?"

Expect disagreements when having this discussion for the first time. You may find that those involved do not agree on who is accountable, responsible etc. The process of doing this is in itself a useful exercise. You may find overlaps and gaps between the responsibilities in your group.

Every Task must have an "A" and an "R" attached to it – they can, of course, relate to the same person.

Once the form starts to be filled out, it can give lots of information at a glance.

"Task 2 will never get done" since nobody is Accountable.

"Why does Fred have to be consulted in all these matters?"

"Who is doing Task 5?"

"What is John actually doing?"

"Who is REALLY in charge of Task 3?"

Etc etc

Once you've had some practice in doing this, you will never NOT set up a RACI diagram for your work, and your life will become easier.

Continuing the journey

Now what?

Do you have everything you need to be a great leader?

I hope this book has helped to make your job easier. Keep it around and refer back to it when you need to.

One of my colleagues, Stuart, used to say that leadership is two things:

- Leadership is a choice.
- Leadership is just a particular kind of relationship.

I believe this is true. Being a leader means that you have chosen to take on a certain kind of relationship with the people you lead. It is up to you to figure out what form this relationship takes.

So, here you are. You have chosen to become a leader. You have some basic tools and some insights into how we all function, you have your own humanity and your personality and frame of reference and inner critic. The rest is just training.

Talk to the people you have chosen to lead. Ask them what they want. Ask for advice. Start a conversation.

Acknowledgements

There are numerous people I have worked with, led, been led by and learned from. Thank you. Some of them deserves a special thank you: Ole, my boss during the good and the tough years in Capgemini; Ninette, my office partner for many years and Kirsten for all the great fights.

My transition into coaching and leadership development was made easier by great coaching, training and camaraderie with Eric and mentoring by Lori.

I've had the privilege of working at many great leadership training programs, I have learned from many people - both trainers, participants and customers. Special thanks to Margo, Stuart, Mimi, Andy, Jim, Marcia, Tony, David, Nick, Ina, Dori, Achim, Angelika, Gabi, Livia, Martina, Peter, Reimar, Robert, Sabine, Uli and Veronika.

People who helped me write this book, read early versions and gave me valuable feedback, with special thanks to Robin.

Friends that I've had great conversations with over many years, with special thanks to Endre and Petter.

Thanks to Joel Cooper, the illustrator.

Very special thanks to the women that supported me the most in writing this book: Lori Shook, my wife and business partner and Sonia Duggan, my editor.

Thank you.

Literature

Books on understanding yourself and others:

Daring Greatly: **Brené Brown**
How the Courage to Be Vulnerable
Transforms the Way We Live, Love,
Parent, and Lead
*About vulnerability. Brown talks about how vulnerability is a
strength, not a weakness.*

Focus: **Daniel Goleman**
The Hidden Driver of Excellence
*Those who excel rely on Smart Practices such as mindfulness
meditation, focused preparation and recovery, positive emotions and
connections, and mental 'prosthetics' that help them improve habits,
add new skills, and sustain excellence.*

Thinking, Fast and Slow   **Daniel Kahneman**
*This book may change the way you think, make better decisions and
be more logical and smarter.*

Incognito: **David Eagleman**
The Secret Lives of The Brain
*Yes, I like to read books about how the brain works, and this is
another fascinating book about the contradictions that happens in
our brain and mind.*

Your Brain at Work   **David Rock**
*Rock shows how it's possible for the reader, not only to survive in
today's overwhelming work environment but succeed in it - and still
feel energized and accomplished at the end of the day.*

Thanks for the Feedback: **Douglas Stone,**
The Science and Art of Receiving Feedback   **Sheila Heen**
Well
*Not often do I read a book that really turns my knowledge (in this
case about feedback) completely upside down. This book is
uncomfortable, but oh! so important.*

The Master and His Emissary: **Iain McGilchrist**
The Divided Brain and the Making of the
Western World
You may have heard about the left and right side of the brain and the differences. This book is great at explaining it but more importantly, discusses the consequences for our lives and culture.

The Psychopath Inside: **James Fallon**
A Neuroscientist's Personal Journey into
the Dark Side of the Brain
Not only will this book help you understand the (small number of) psychopaths out there, but also your own brain better.

The Well-Tuned Brain: **Peter C. Whybrow**
Neuroscience and the Life Well Lived
This is a book on the bigger questions: What kind of future do we want to create for this planet? How can we use our newfound knowledge about the brain to make better choices?

Taming Your Gremlin   **Richard David**
A Surprisingly Simple Method for Getting   **Carson**
Out of Your Own Way
This is a great book about how to get over your inner critic (your gremlin), the negative chatter that gets in your own way.

Sapiens: **Yuval Noah**
A Brief History of Humankind   **Harari**
Sapiens is a thrilling account of humankind's extraordinary history – from the Stone Age to the Silicon Age – and our journey from insignificant apes to rulers of the world.

Books on Leadership and organisations:

Holacracy: Brian J.
The Revolutionary Management System   Robertson
that Abolishes Hierarchy
A radical way of organizing a company, and how to overcome the challenges of this new way of operating.

Switch: How to change things when change   Chip Heath,
is hard   Dan Heath
Looking at how our brain works, in order to get better at managing change.

The Way of the Peaceful Warrior: Dan Millman
A Book That Changes Lives
Tells a great story about a successful guy who finds even more meaning and purpose in his life. I liked it a lot, even if I'm not so much of a spiritual reader.

Tribal Leadership: Dave Logan,
Leveraging Natural Groups to Build a   John King
Thriving Organization
We – as human beings – form tribes and this book shows how the tribes develop and how we can utilize the power of tribes.

Reinventing Organizations: Frederic Laloux
A Guide to Creating Organizations
Inspired by the Next Stage of Human
Consciousness
Radical stuff! Looking at profoundly new ways of organizing ourselves. Laloux takes us on a journey through history, and shows how different levels of enlightenment create different organisations.

Living Leadership: George Binney,
A Practical Guide for Ordinary Heroes   Colin Williams
Living Leadership explodes the myth of the charismatic, transformational leader, to show that real progress comes from the dramatically ordinary aspects of leadership.

Training on Trial: James D.
How Workplace Learning Must Reinvent   Kirkpatrick
Itself to Remain Relevant
The authors rocked a lot of my own conceptions and myths about training in organisations.

The Seven Principles for Making Marriage Work: John M. Gottman

This is not only about marriages! Gottman looks at different kinds of relationships and what makes them stronger – or weaker.

Leadership and the One Minute Manager   Kenneth Blanchard

If you have heard the term "Situational Leadership", this is where to find it explained.

The Tipping Point: Malcolm Gladwell
How Little Things Can Make a Big Difference

I like the books by Malcolm Gladwell. Well written, fun and thought-provoking. This is about that magic moment when ideas, trends and social behaviour cross a threshold, tip and spread like wildfire.

The Five Dysfunctions of a Team,   Patrick M.
A Leadership Fable   Lencioni

This book is useful to understand how leadership teams can vastly improve performance if they understand their five typical dysfunctions.

The Fear-free Organization: Paul Brown,
Vital Insights from Neuroscience to   Joan Kinsley,
Transform Your Business Culture   Sue Paterson

It's easy to see that scared people will not be high performers, but this book gives great explanations as to why and how we should strive for a fear-free work environment.

Books on coaching:

Co-active Coaching: **New Skills for Coaching People** **Toward Success in Work and Life**	**Laura Whitworth,** **Henry Kimsey-House,** **Phil Sandahl**

The definite book on co-active coaching from the founders of the school where I got my first coaching education.

Challenging Coaching: Going Beyond **Traditional Coaching to Face the** **FACTS**	**John Blakey**

Using the FACTS coaching model, Feedback, Accountability, Courageous goals, Tension, and Systems thinking, and adapting a more challenging coaching stance to get better results.

Coaching for Performance: GROWing **Human Potential and Purpose - the** **Principles and Practice of Coaching** **and Leadership**	**John Whitmore**

A classic book on coaching, how to unlock other people's potential. Explains in detail the GROW model.

There Is an I in Team: **What Elite Athletes and Coaches** **Really Know About High Performance**	**Mark de Rond,** **Richard Hytner**

How to work with the dilemma: you need strong individuals for high performance, but these individuals might negatively impact the performance of the team.

Other great books:

The Brothers Lionheart   **Astrid Lindgren**
I grew up with Astrid Lindgren's children books, and this one still fascinates me. About the courage we all have inside.

Born to Run: **Christopher**
The hidden tribe, the ultra-runners, and the   **McDougall**
greatest race the world has never seen
I didn't really become a runner until after I turned 50. This book was one of the reasons I started to run.

Alan Turing: **David Boyle**
Unlocking the Enigma
I love reading books about underdogs, outcasts and outliers. Alan Turing qualifies. His contributions to our modern world should not be overlooked.

South: **Sir Ernest Henry**
The Story of Shackleton's   **Shackleton**
1914-1917 Expedition
Being Norwegian, I used to frown upon Shackleton's fiasco. Then I read his story and changed my perspective. A true hero and a great leader.

Animal Farm   **George Orwell**
It's one of those books that are often referred to, and quoted from. I've read it a couple of times, and still think we should take learning from Orwell's fable.

Long Walk to Freedom   **Nelson Mandela**
I admit: Mandela was one of my heroes from young age. I visited his cell on Robben Island and then I read his biography. I wish I did it in reverse order.

Lord of the Flies   **William Golding**
What happens when rules and regulations, police, the thin layer of civilization and culture are removed? The story of young boys stranded on an island speaks to me about the situation in the world today.

www.ingramcontent.com/pod-product-compliance
Lightning Source LLC
Chambersburg PA
CBHW070806180526
45168CB00002B/511